1002 WAYS TO

WASTE

YOUR

WORKING

TIME

THE DIAGRAM GROUP

St. Martin's Griffin ❧ New York

A THOMAS DUNNE BOOK.
An imprint of St. Martin's Press.

1002 WAYS TO WASTE YOUR WORKING TIME. Copyright © 1996 by The Diagram Group. All rights reserved. Printed in the United States of America. No part of this book may be used or reproduced in any manner whatsoever without written permission except in the case of brief quotations embodied in critical articles or reviews. For information, address St. Martin's Press, 175 Fifth Avenue, New York, N.Y. 10010.

Library of Congress Cataloging-in-Publication Data

1002 ways to waste your working time / by the Diagram Group.
   p. cm.
  "A Thomas Dunne Book"
  ISBN 0-312-14534-9
  1. Work—humor. 2. Time management—humor. I. Diagram Group.
PN6231.W44A17 1996   96-22607
828'.9140208—dc20   CIP

First St. Martin's Griffin Edition: September 1996

10 9 8 7 6 5 4 3 2 1

Introduction

- This subject is not taught at any school or college, but strangely these places are breeding grounds for many of the ideas. Pupils from the age of five onward are quick to develop, without any help from their teachers, time-wasting skills that can serve them well in later life.

- This book is not the work of one man or woman – rather it is the compilation of a lifetime of research by members of the Diagram Group, whose efforts to discover how to avoid work have not always met with success.

- Many have failed and have spent their working life doing worthwhile tasks. Only a few have succeeded in discovering their own ways to achieve the goal of TIME WASTING.

- Wherever in the world people have to work, and whatever work they do, they will find this book useful in helping them to avoid completing the tasks.

- WARNING: This book should not be used as an idea source for the time you have available for leisure. It is strictly intended for assistance with those hours in which you should be gainfully employed in work.

- As with most scientific endeavors, all of the activities in this book have been tested in varying conditions to prove their validity and effectiveness.

- This book has been compiled from over one million hours of research. Nevertheless, with the best will in the world, and in spite of deep dedication, the researchers may have missed valuable activities that could be pursued in the search for ways to waste time.

- The research is continuing.

- Should you have your own effective time-wasting methods, please send a list of a minimum of fifty to Diagram so that other devotees can benefit from your discoveries.

The Diagram Group
195 Kentish Town Road
London NW5 8SY
England
Fax no. +44 171 482 4932

Credits
Designer – Darren Bennett
Artists – Dipna Majhu, Kyri Kyriacou

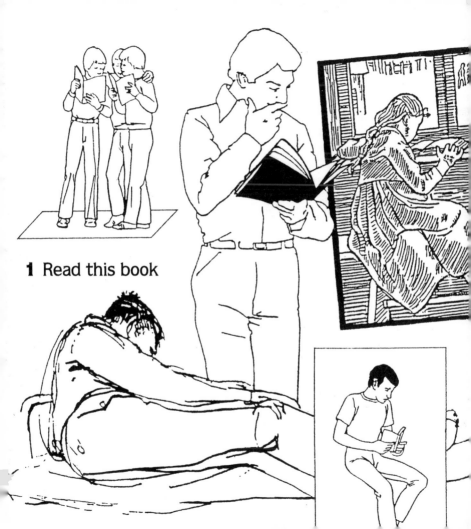

1 Read this book

2 Count the number of checks left in your checkbook

3 Look at old diaries to see what you did this time last year and the year before

4 Make a rubbing of a coin

5 Straighten the wire clothes hangers in the closet

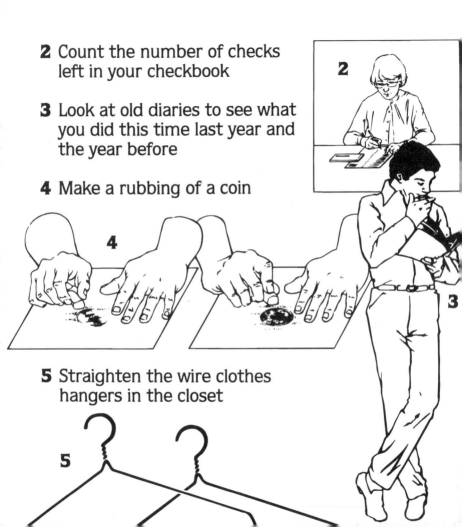

6 Read an old *TV Guide*

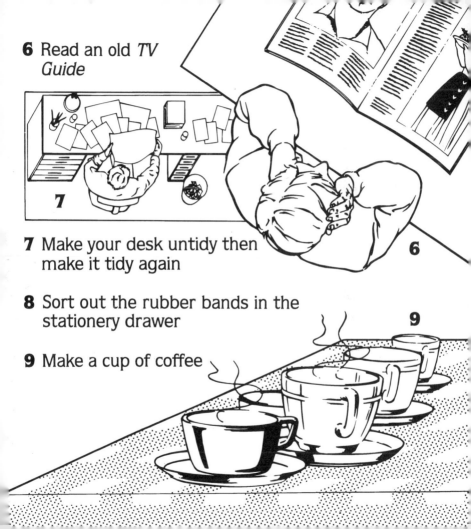

7 Make your desk untidy then make it tidy again

8 Sort out the rubber bands in the stationery drawer

9 Make a cup of coffee

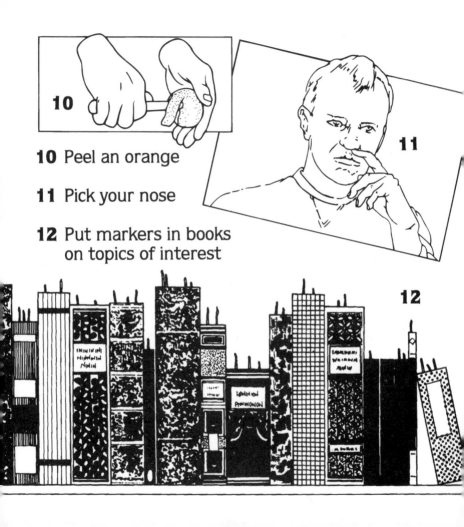

10 Peel an orange

11 Pick your nose

12 Put markers in books on topics of interest

13 Wash your hands

14 Torment the cat

15 Read the ingredients on a sauce bottle

16 Pick off old nail polish

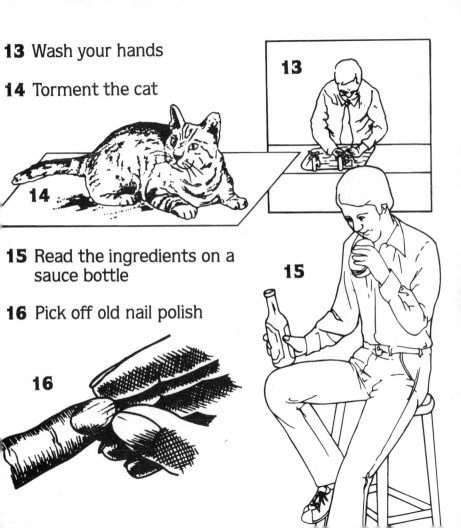

17 Draw mustaches onto photos in magazines

18 Practice blowing smoke rings

19 Sort out all your used envelopes

20 Straighten the picture on the wall

17

20

21 Retie your shoelaces

22 Water the plants

23 Untangle the cords on your blinds

24 Scratch your arm where it is not itching

25 Make faces at the goldfish

26 Wind up your watch

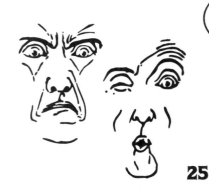

27 Practice different handwriting styles

28 Squeeze the zits on your face

29 Copy out your list of "tasks to do" again in a neat form

30 Arrange unpaid bills by date order

31 Play with worry beads

32 Get your calculator to spell words

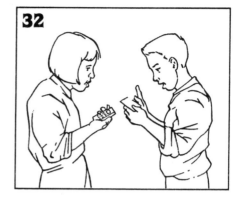

33 Read your horoscope in an old newspaper

34 Invent an office golf obstacle course

35 Make a paper hat from office stationery

36 Rearrange the boardroom furniture

37 Create shadow figures using your hands

GOAT

DO...

DU...

SHE...

38 Make ten words from your name using each letter just once

39

39 Try to recall the periodic table

40 Try to remember the order of the Ten Commandments

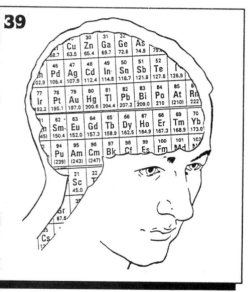

Darren
Bennett
aeee bdnnr

ten   ten
net   ren
bad   de
read   br
drab   br

41 Hold your head in your hands

42 Practice forging your boss's signature

43 Visit a friend

44 Try to remember the Gettysburg Address

45 Tell someone a spooky campfire tale

46 Search for faces in the wallpaper

47 Walk up and down

50

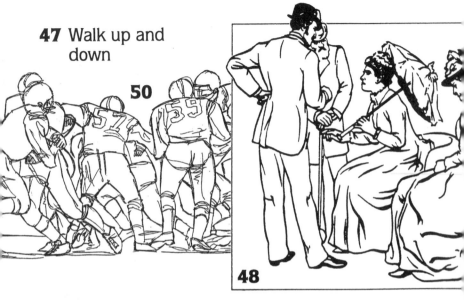

48

48 Make a list of
people you should invite to dinner

49 Plan a bank robbery

50 Predict which football team will win
this year's Super Bowl

51 Work out your weight in kilos

52 Check your house price from the real estate advertisements in the local paper

53 Browse through *Roget's Thesaurus*

54 Make a parcel of unwanted objects and send it to someone in a different department

55 Find out what is on TV this week

56 Play with a hole in your teeth with your tongue

57 Make a list of anagrams from your name

58 Plan to dispose of a body

59 Make your own crossword puzzle

60 Try to see down your throat with a mirror

61 Try to remember the license plate numbers of all the cars you have ever owned

59

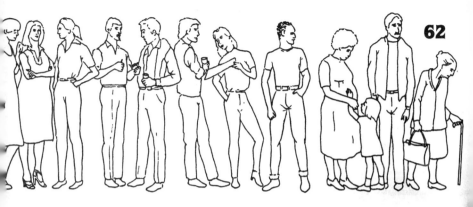

62 Invent personalities for each of the people in this picture

63 Make a list of ten questions you would ask Napoleon should you meet in the afterlife

64 Practice balancing a dime on its edge

65 Plan what you would do with only ten hours to live

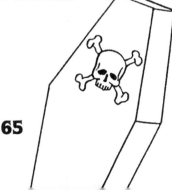

65

66 Figure out how to use color in a map with the minimum number of colors so that no two adjacent areas are the same color

66

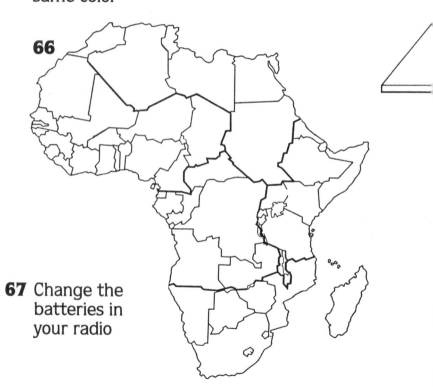

67 Change the batteries in your radio

68 Work out your height in meters

69 Try to pick up small objects using crossed fingers

70 Test the pens on your desk

71 Make a shopping list for next Christmas

72 Try to slide as far down a chair as possible without falling off

73 Cut an envelope to make scrap paper

74 Tidy your office drawers

75 Do a "head-over-heels"

76 Invent characters for a novel

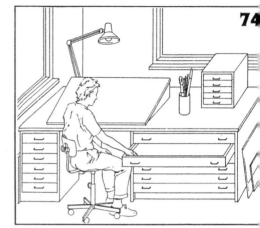

77 Practice writing your signature left-handed

78 Decide where to go on vacation next year

79 Think about sex

80 Trim your nose hairs

78

81 Work out what time it is in Tokyo

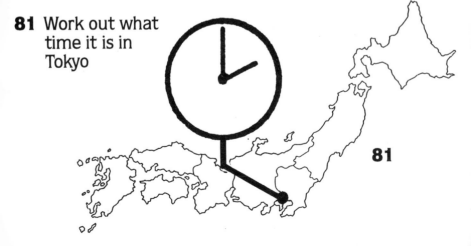

81

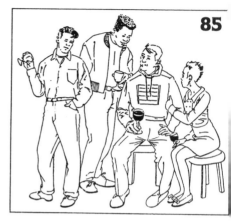

82 Write words in the mist formed by your breath on a cold window or mirror

83 Go out and buy a pack of cigarettes

84 Make silhouette cutouts of your workmates

85 Invite friends out for a drink after work

86 Read your own fortune in a teacup

87 Figure out if you can climb through a playing card

88 Conduct an imaginary orchestra

89 Have a snack

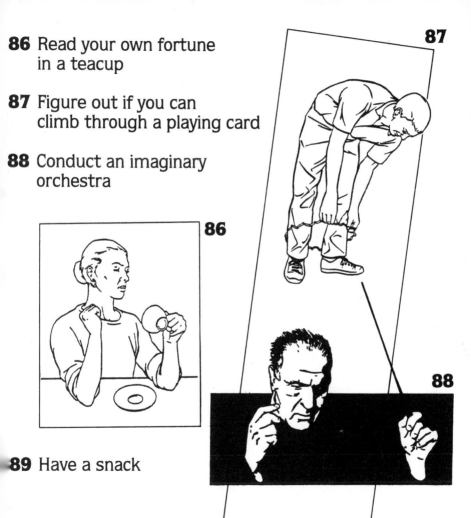

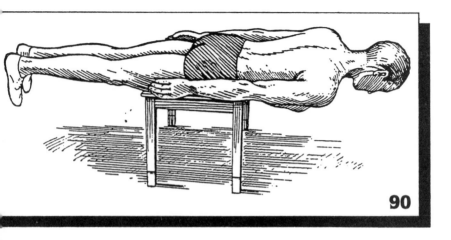

90 Practice your swimming skills by lying across a stool

91 Type an anonymous letter to someone and send it through inter-office mail

92 Clean out your ear with a Q-Tip

93 Look at your vacation photos

94 Guess how much and then count the money in your pockets

95 Call someone whose name begins with the letter "L"

96 Sit and stare

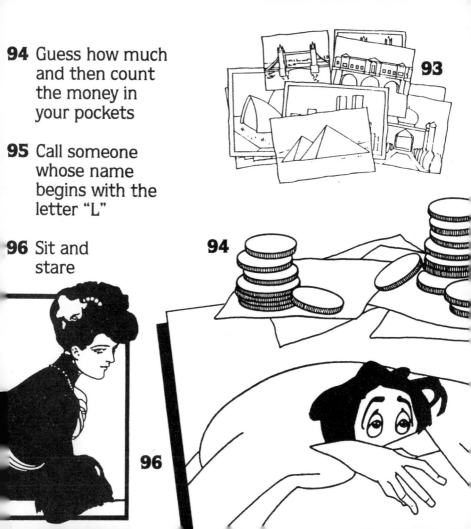

97 Touch your toes

98 Make a list of things that you would pack to take on a vacation to Hawaii

99 Play yourself at tick-tack-toe

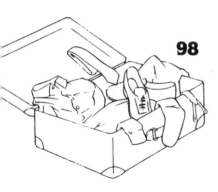

98

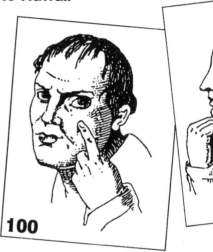

100

101

100 Change the proportions of your face

101 Pretend you are a statue

102 Doze in a chair

97

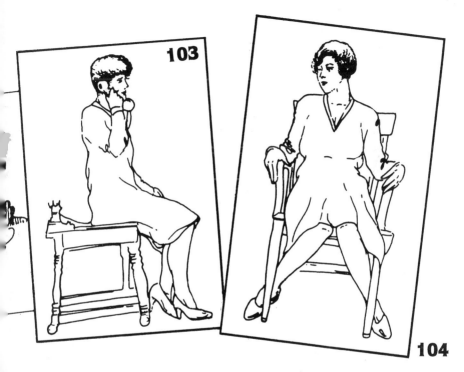

03 Pretend you are speaking to someone on the phone

04 Twist your legs around the chair in which you are sitting

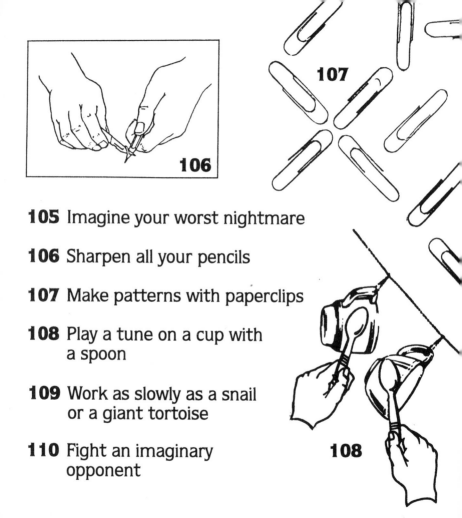

105 Imagine your worst nightmare

106 Sharpen all your pencils

107 Make patterns with paperclips

108 Play a tune on a cup with a spoon

109 Work as slowly as a snail or a giant tortoise

110 Fight an imaginary opponent

111 Sing arias from operas very loudly, waving your arms around at the same time

111

12 Try to recall your earliest thoughts

13 Sit and cross and uncross your legs

14 Study a map of a region you are unlikely to ever visit

15 Have a cold beer

112

115

116 Try to find a baby-sitter and arrange a night out

117 Fold brown paper into neat squares

118 Distort a picture of you or a friend on the company photocopier

118

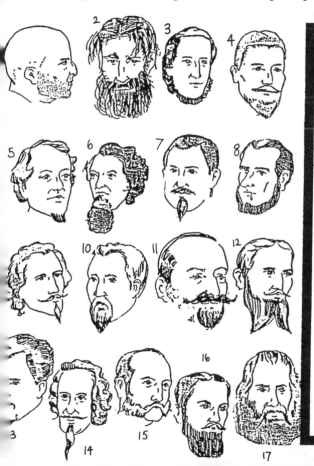

1. Stubble
2. unkept-natural
3. saucer or trencher or Captain Ahab
4. goatee
5. breakwater
6. Uncle Sam
7. bodkin
8. trimmed (shaven upper lip)
9. vandyke
10. spade
11. handlebar and goatee
12. forked
13. marquessate
14. stiletto
15. burnsides
16. square cut
17. bush

120 Try to remember where you put last year's Christmas list

120

121 Lie horizontal on the floor

122 See what your name spells when you write it backward

122

123 Remove hairs from your clothes

124 Clear out the hole punch

124

PAUL - LUAP
LISA - ASI
STEVE - EVE
NICOLE - EL
CHRIS - S

125 Clean up the mess after clearing out the hole punch

126 Think of how you would fire someone if you were the boss

127 Check the classified ads in the paper to see if there is anything you need

128 Phone up someone in the company you do not know and say hello

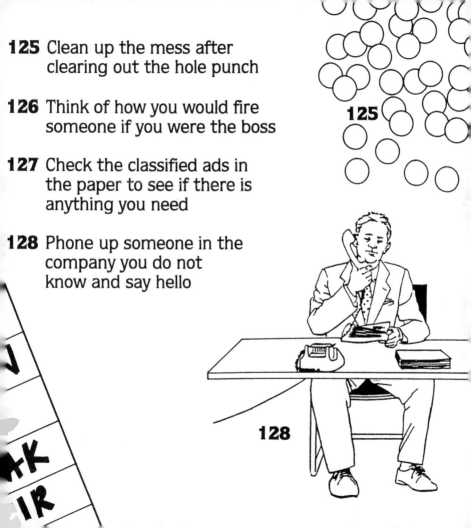

129 See how many different positions you can get your desk lamp to go in

130 Clean your shoes

131 Fill out the personal notes page of your office calendar

132 Practice throwing crumpled up pieces of paper into the wastepaper basket

133 Change the order of your keys on your key ring

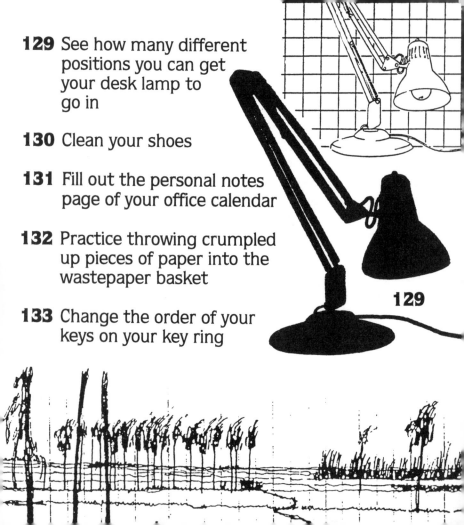

129

134 Borrow a pen from someone in another office

135 Clear out the company medicine cabinet

136 Think of a spot in the countryside you have longed to visit

37 Imagine yourself as an artist painting your dream house

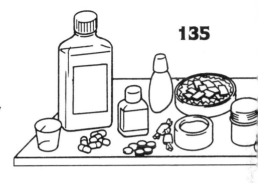

135

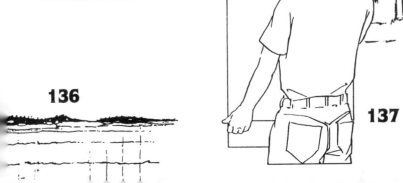

136

137

138 Make sure that the birthdays of all your family and friends are listed in your office calendar

139 Think what you would do with three wishes from your very own genie

140 Imagine riding home through traffic on a penny-farthing

141 Take all the dead matches out of matchboxes

139

140

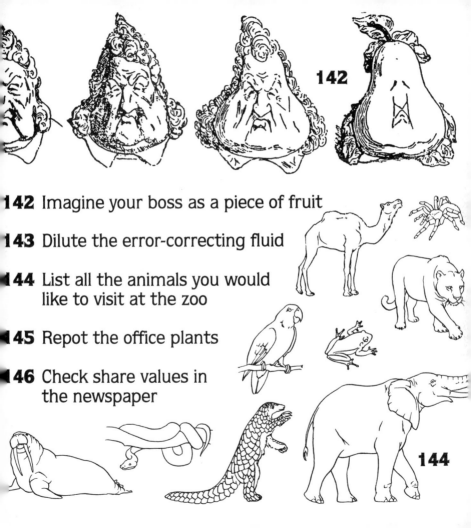

142 Imagine your boss as a piece of fruit

143 Dilute the error-correcting fluid

144 List all the animals you would like to visit at the zoo

145 Repot the office plants

146 Check share values in the newspaper

147 Close your eyes and imagine what it would be like to be blind

148 Think about how lonely astronauts must feel up in space

148

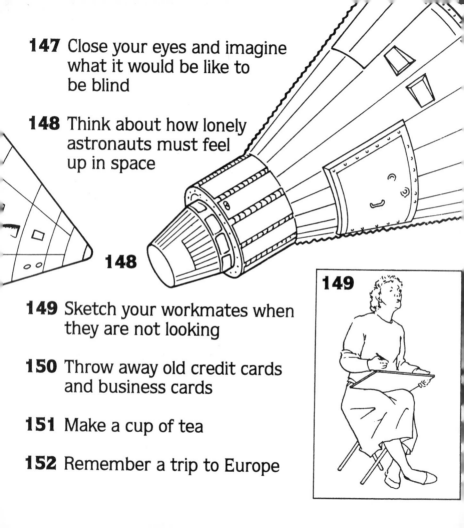

149 Sketch your workmates when they are not looking

150 Throw away old credit cards and business cards

151 Make a cup of tea

152 Remember a trip to Europe

53 Plan a trip to Europe if you have not been there

54 Put the books on your shelf in order of subject

55 Call up someone you talked to last year

56 Arrange to meet a friend in the washroom to chat

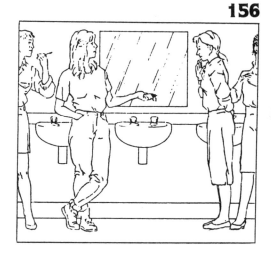

61 Phone someone in your office to see if they are bored

62 Pick your teeth with a toothpick

164

161

63 Watch a friend work

64 Try to imagine what your children are doing

165 Imagine making a living by loaning people money

166 Read the acknowledgments of a book

167 Try to look at the end of your nose

168 Talk to the office plants

169 Remember times when you were at the beach as a child

167

165

169

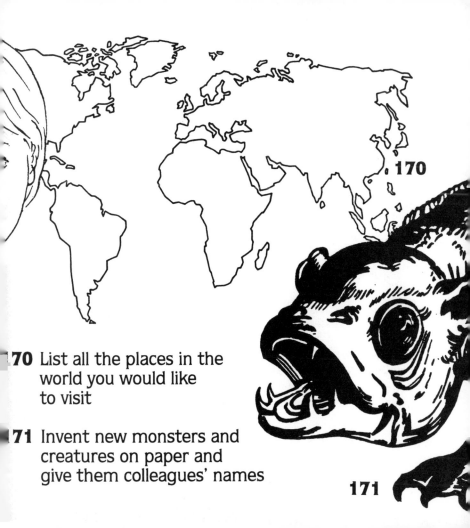

170 List all the places in the world you would like to visit

171 Invent new monsters and creatures on paper and give them colleagues' names

172 Imagine being very rich. **173** Calculate how much money you spend each year. **174** Build a ladder of good intentions to Heaven. **175** Invent a conversation between Napoleon and Hitler. **176** Practice levitating. **177** Play an imaginary harmonica. **178** Draw a totem pole using the faces of colleagues and friends. **179** Show colleagues cartoons of your boss. **180** Hop on one leg along a straight line. **181** Blow your own imaginary trumpet. **182** Imagine what you would say to someone – a friend or relative – who returns from the dead. **183** Imagine what you would do with ultimate power. **184** Pretend to dance around the room with Fred Astaire. **185** Imagine how you would escape from being tied up. **186** Think of a new use for a strange tool. **187** Remember your first kiss.

175

172

173

188 Make a list of your best features. **189** Imagine an orgy. **190** Play your boss at checkers. **191** Imagine pressing hot kisses onto the one you love. **192** Frighten a friend. **193** Imagine a perfect murder. **194** Figure the values of half and half and half a number until you arrive at its twentieth value. **195** Console a colleague. **196** Invent ways of disposing of a body. **197** Pretend to be dead and lie very still. **198** Dream of possessing your loved one. **199** Eat strange food that will keep you awake all night and make you feel so tired that tomorrow you will fall asleep. **200** Imagine the colors of fairies' wings. **201** Enact a dog fight in the sky between two airplanes, using your hands to describe the actions, and making machine gun noises with your mouth.

199

195

187

202 Study the controls of a space shuttle so you can pi
the ship back to earth

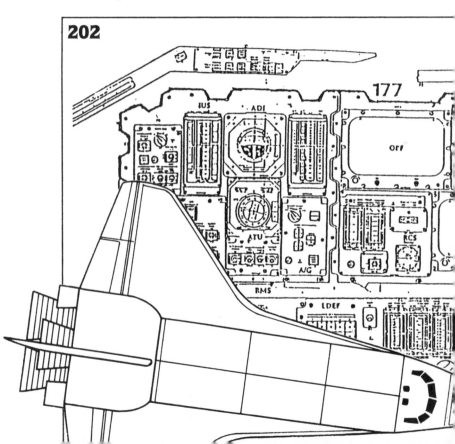

203 Stand holding a chair and swing alternate
legs backward and forward

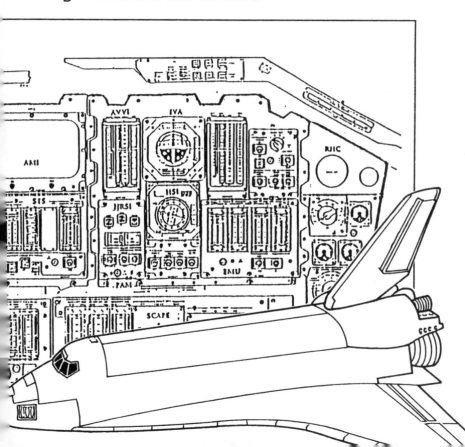

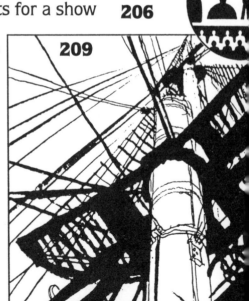

211

211 Send someone you love a gift

212 Imagine what is "going on" next door

214

213 Flick paper at friends

214 Rehearse your excuses for when you are caught in an embarrassing situation

215 Practice insulting hand gestures

216 Carve your initials onto your desk

217 Pull down your cuffs and fiddle with the buttons

218 Twiddle your thumbs

219 Imagine being taken away by a superhero

220 Do exercises in your chair

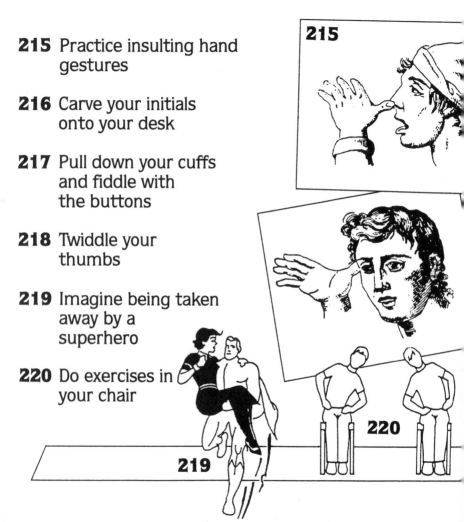

221 Imagine working in a tower in a castle

222 Fiddle with your earring

223 Raise hell

221

222

24 Brush back your hair with your left hand

225 Fold and refold your handkerchief

226 Invent families for these people

227 Play with the keys or money in your pocket

228 Imagine how sorry everyone will be when you are dead

229 Say "Oh, dear me" repeatedly

230 Pretend you are a race car driver

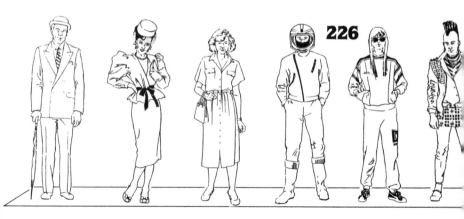

226

231 Clean out the sleep from your eyes

232 Describe what Lincoln might be thinking
if he were not a statue

236

239 Sort out old newspapers and magazines

240 Think of a comic you read as a child

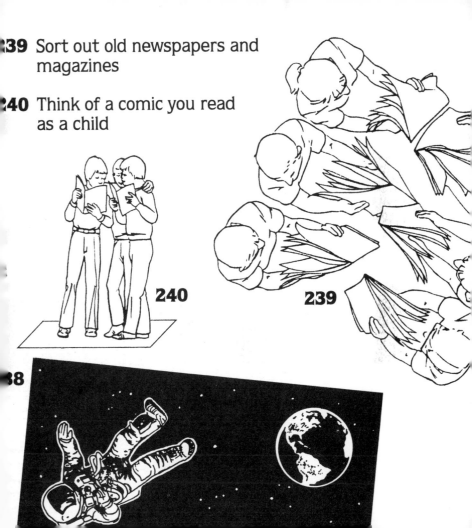

240

239

38

241 Count the buttons on your jacket

242 Imagine what you would look like with no hair

243 Read any section of a dull book

244 Scratch a spot

245 Invent new items for a later edition of this book

246 Play cards with a colleague

247 Make funny faces at the person nearest you

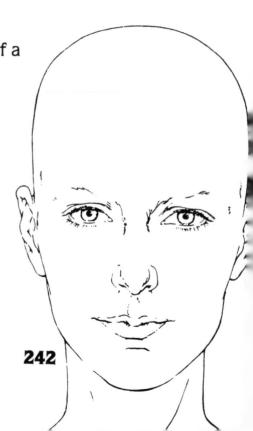

242

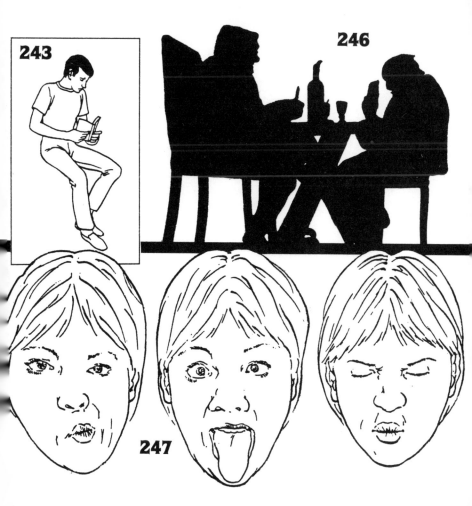

243

246

247

248 Invent a correspondence with someone famous

248

249 Turn out your pockets and brush off the fluff

250 Make a paper airplane

251 Throw your paper airplane to someone, if you haven't already

252 Imagine your living room with new wallpaper

252

253 Read a map of the places you will never go to

254 Empty your pockets

255 Imagine colleagues' reactions if you came to work dressed differently

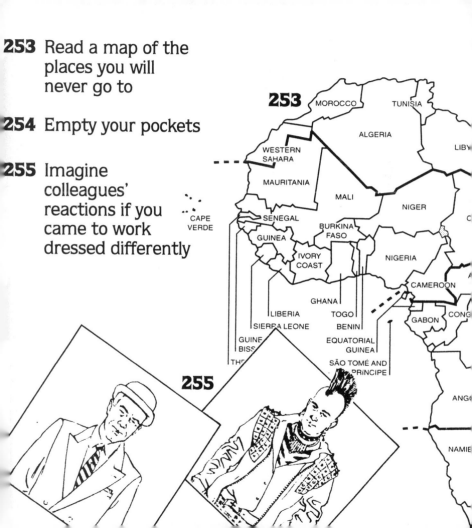

256 Smoke pot in the storeroom

25

257 Try to remember who got drunk at the office party

258 Put cotton balls in your ears and imagine you are deaf

259 Boil water and make a cup of tea

260 Draw a Ouija board and try to contact the original chairperson of your company

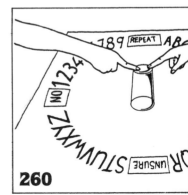

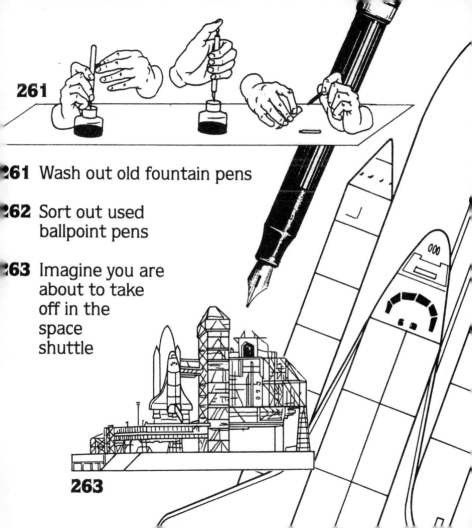

261 Wash out old fountain pens

262 Sort out used ballpoint pens

263 Imagine you are about to take off in the space shuttle

263

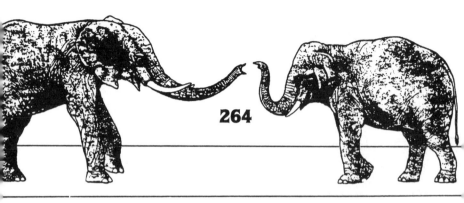

264

264 Convince someone that an African elephant has smaller ears than an Asian elephant

265 Calculate your monthly expenses

266 Go to the bathroom

267 Have a cigarette

265

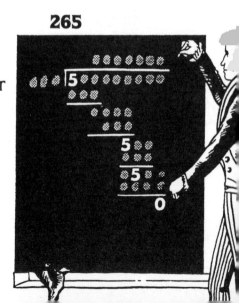

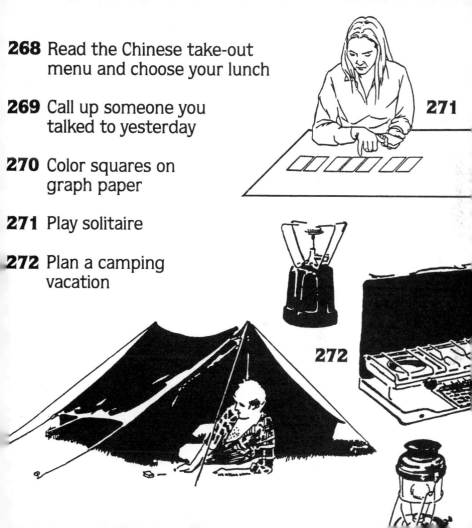

268 Read the Chinese take-out menu and choose your lunch

269 Call up someone you talked to yesterday

270 Color squares on graph paper

271 Play solitaire

272 Plan a camping vacation

274

275

276 Clean your fingernails

277 Remember an old friend

278 Tease a workmate

279 Read a tourist brochure

280 Draw glasses on faces in today's newspaper

281 Do some knitting

282 Put your name in all the books on the shelf

283 Search your hair for lice

284 Rearrange tapes

285 Make a list of things to do on the weekend

286 Fill in earlier weeks in your office calendar

287 Fill in your office calendar with things you would like to be doing

287

MONDAY	TUESDAY	WEDNESDAY T
week.1. Go to the cinema	Stay bed in all day!	Phone in sick and spend a day at home
week.2. Visit a friend in Newquay	Invite friends round for a meal	Have strawberries and cream, and champagne for break
Spend a day in the countryside	Go to a jazz concert	Watch the football on TV with friends

288 Imagine what child care is like for male seahorses. **289** Rub your tummy while tapping your head. **290** Doze. **291** Practice writing a letter without looking at the paper. **292** Imagine standing next to the tallest tree in the world. **293** Figure the relationship between extraterrestrial forces, metaphysical forces, paranormal forces, and the orders of spiritual levels in Heaven and Hell. **294** Imagine two whales making love in the ocean. **295** Sit and think about why you work where you do. **296** Calculate all the money you have spent in your life so far. **297** Do sit-ups on the floor. **298** Play music to your plants. **299** Consult an oracle. **300** Peep through a keyhole at an office meeting. **301** Imagine reading a diary of several past generations written by your great-grandmother.

288

294

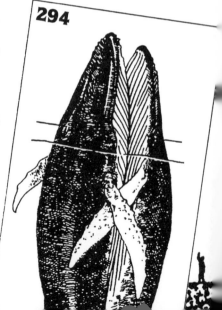

296

302 Imagine working in a pit crew for a racing team. **303** Calculate how long it would take you to read a twenty-volume encyclopedia. **304** Imagine being thin. **305** Check your make-up in a small mirror. **306** Consult a book to interpret your dreams. **307** Tell someone to calm down. **308** Draw your own profile. **309** Watch a friend working and mimic their habits. **310** Figure out the largest single sum of money you ever earned. **311** Figure out the largest single sum of money you ever paid anyone. **312** Throw a fit. **313** In the two pictures shown upside down against each other, figure out the differences. **314** Remember all the people at your bus stop on the way to work. **315** Hold your breath. **316** Think what you could do with three extra fingers. **317** Prune and shape the company bonsai tree.

313

304

317

318 Rethink what was said to you yesterday

319 Plan a night out with your best friends at your favorite restaurant

320 String together rubber bands

321 Lean back in your chair and look at the ceiling

322 Think of the day you got married

323 Imagine what it would be like to be a fish in the sea

324 Try to remember the tune of the *Warsaw Concerto*

323

324

22

325 Draw up a two-month calendar and add special events

326 Try to remember the name of the tiny man in *The Maltese Falcon*

327 Remember your first day at work

328 Try to remember the formula for the volume of a sphere

329 Approach someone at work you don't know and say hello

330 Think of something you would prefer to be doing now

331 Swing on your chair

332 Pretend to hold a gun and shoot people as they walk by

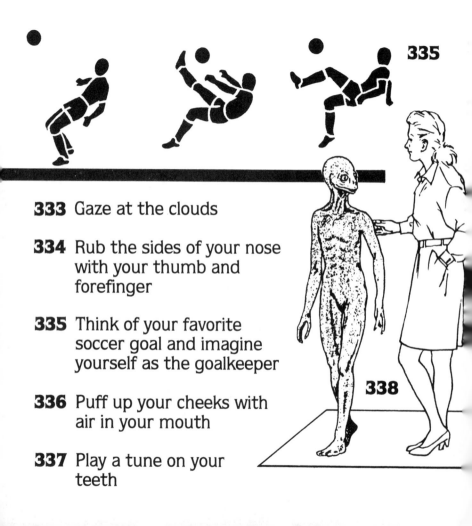

333 Gaze at the clouds

334 Rub the sides of your nose with your thumb and forefinger

335 Think of your favorite soccer goal and imagine yourself as the goalkeeper

336 Puff up your cheeks with air in your mouth

337 Play a tune on your teeth

338 Invent the conversation you might have if you met with an alien

339 Imagine what you will do when you retire

340 Count the stars

341 Imagine what you will do between now and your retirement

342 Describe the last days in the lives of the dinosaurs that made these fossils

343 Play a tune with your tongue (make galloping sounds)

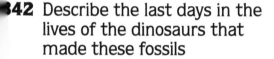

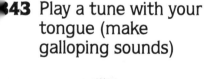

344 Whistle out a tune

345 Think of ten reasons why you should not get married

346 Imagine a discussion with a drunk

347

347 Flip a coin to see who gets the coffee at break

348 Clean out the supply closet

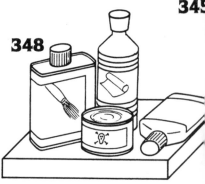

348

345

349 Try to recall the names of kids in your elementary school

350 Push back the cuticles on your nails

351 Think who you would take away with you for a dream weekend

352 Crack your knuckles

353 Think of a new route to get to work

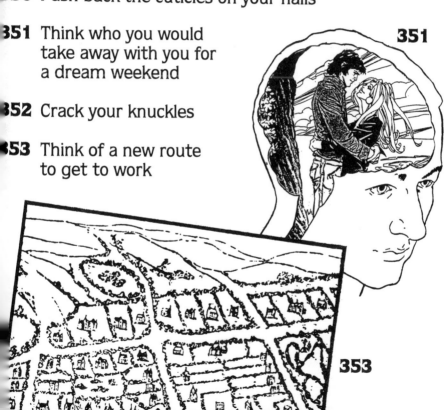

351

353

354 Make a "Big Brother" poster of your boss using the photocopier

355 Imagine life if you were as small as a cat

356 Refill your staple gun

357 Invent a day in the life of a small dinosaur

358 Work out how to spend this week's paycheck

359 Think of all the things you can sell that you don't really need

360 Decide what style of topiary you would like in your garden

361 Find out how to adopt an animal at the zoo

362 Get someone's attention by kicking them in the backside

363 Make a paperclip chain

360

362

364 Try to remember who was the class "brain" when you were fifteen years old

365 Pick a day to take your children to the park

366 Play a card trick on a friend

366

367 Invent a new animal using the characteristics of three existing ones

365

367

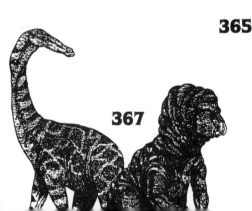

368 Learn five new words in your dictionary

369 Take the bulb out of your desk lamp and replace it

370 Chat to a workmate about the book you are reading

371 Draw a cartoon of a close friend

372 Describe to a colleague how you would explain to a child how a baby is made

373 Think about how big this dinosaur's toes might have been after seeing its thigh bone

373

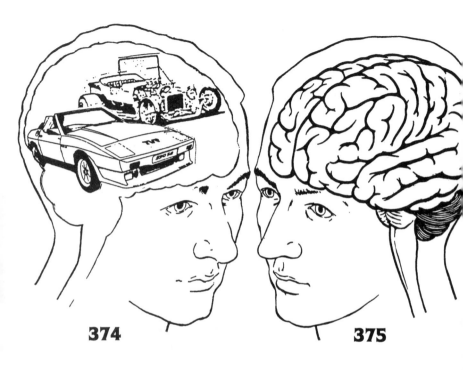

374 Work out how to pay for your dream car

375 Test your IQ

376 Imagine how cold it would be living in an igloo

377 Sing a song in the style of your favorite popstar

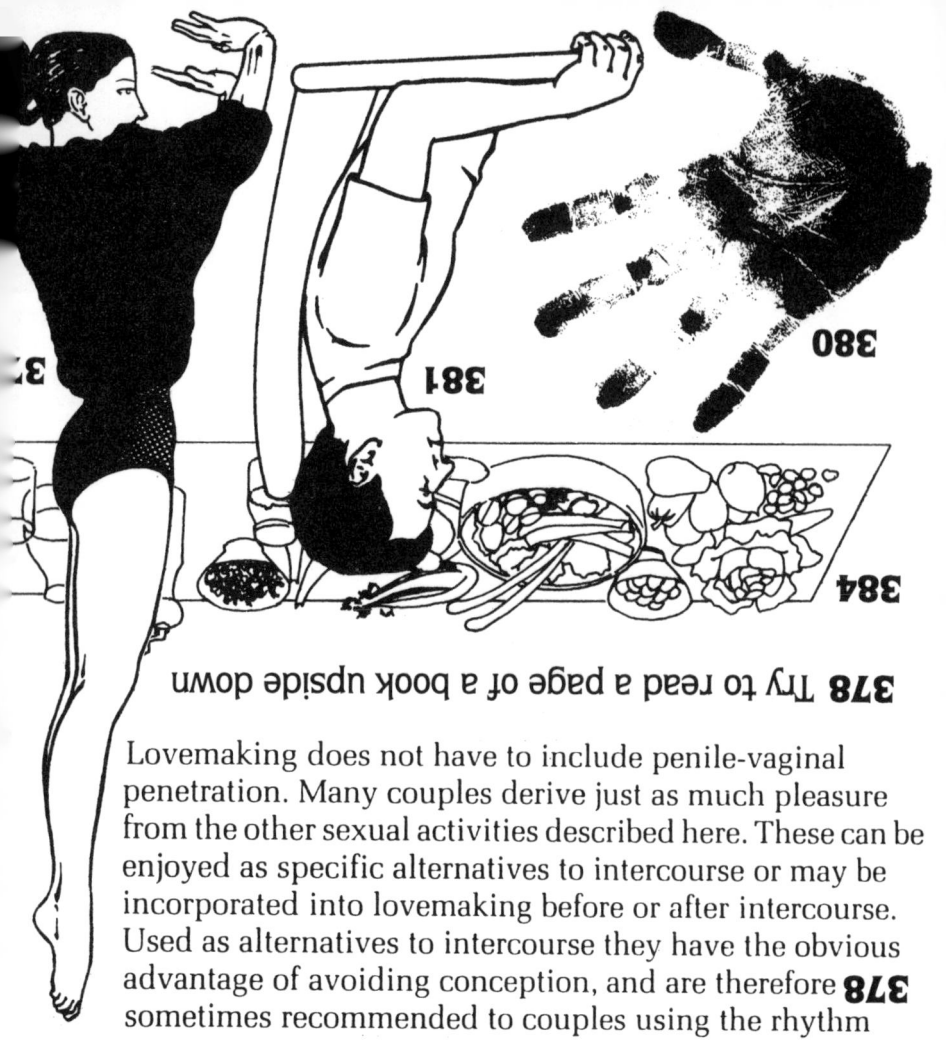

378 Try to read a page of a book upside down

Lovemaking does not have to include penile-vaginal penetration. Many couples derive just as much pleasure from the other sexual activities described here. These can be enjoyed as specific alternatives to intercourse or may be incorporated into lovemaking before or after intercourse. Used as alternatives to intercourse they have the obvious advantage of avoiding conception, and are therefore **378** sometimes recommended to couples using the rhythm

379 Stand on your head

380 Photocopy your hand

381 Listen to the radio

382 Split a pencil to see if you can get the lead out in one piece

383

383 Watch the clouds to see which way the wind is blowing

384 Plan what you will cook for dinner this evening

385 Try and remember your parents' zip code

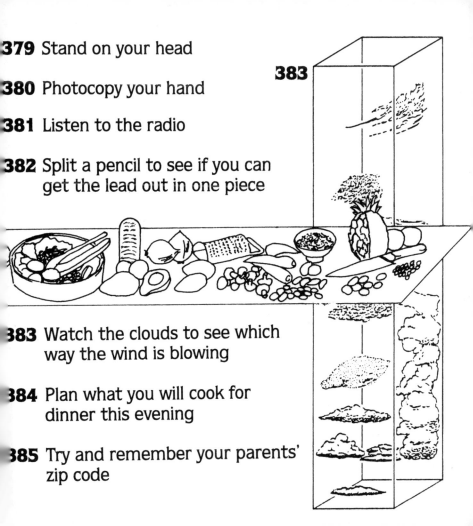

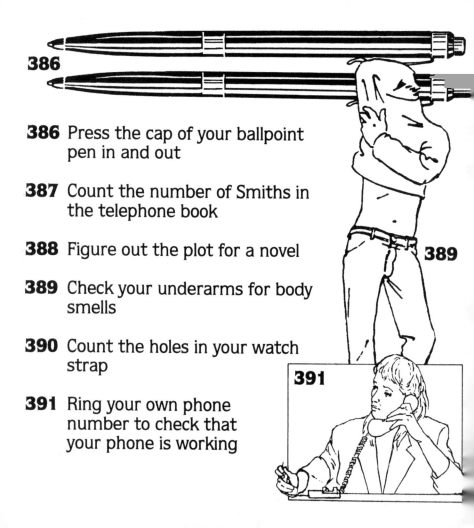

386 Press the cap of your ballpoint pen in and out

387 Count the number of Smiths in the telephone book

388 Figure out the plot for a novel

389 Check your underarms for body smells

390 Count the holes in your watch strap

391 Ring your own phone number to check that your phone is working

392 Chew the end of a ballpoint pen

393 Draw out your family tree

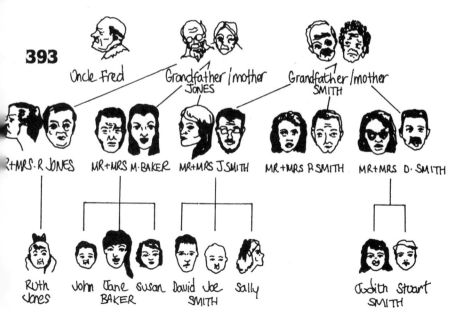

393

Uncle Fred

Grandfather/mother JONES

Grandfather/mother SMITH

R+MRS. R JONES

MR+MRS M. BAKER

MR+MRS J. SMITH

MR+MRS P. SMITH

MR+MRS D. SMITH

Ruth Jones

John Jane Susan BAKER

David Joe SMITH

Sally

Judith Stuart SMITH

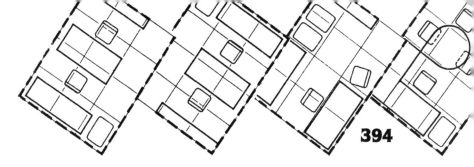

394 Re-arrange the workspace

395 Look to see if anything has fallen behind the radiators

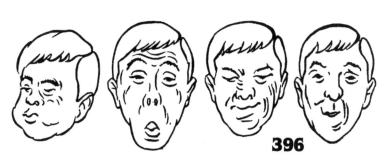

396

396 Twist your face into different shapes

401

397 Make a list of all the people you'd enjoy having sex with

398 See how many words you can make from your own full name

399 Take up yoga

400 Make a list of the ten most attractive women in the world

401 Count the small change in your pockets or purse

402 See how long you can hold your breath

403 Make a list of the ten most attractive men in the world

404 Add up your debts

405 Imagine how you would pick a fight with your friends

402

404

405

406 Imagine what people will be reading about in a year's time

407 Look through last year's staff party photographs

408 Work out the perfect murder

409 See how far down a chair you can slide before you fall to the ground

410 Make a musical instrument from a paper and comb

411 Make a list of the ten best films ever made

412 Make a list of the ten people you would arrest immediately if you became dictator

413 Walk around the building looking busy

414 Plan how to give up smoking or any vice

415 Try to see the minute hand of your watch moving

416 Drum out a rhythm with your fingers

1.

2.

3.

4.

5.

417 Make a list of your replies in answer to questions about your work colleagues so the lie detector does not reveal your true feelings

412

414

417

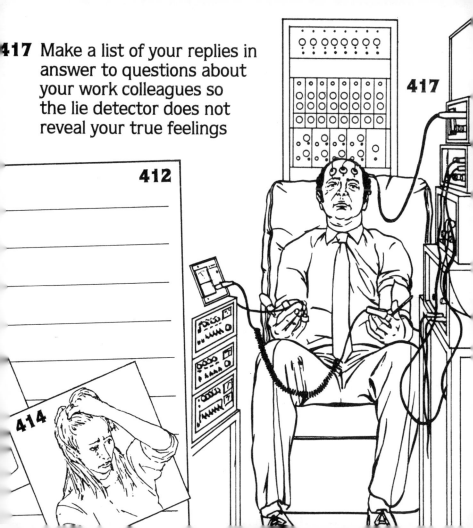

418 Work out how much you could save if you gave up smoking or other activities

419 Try to wiggle your toes

420 Try a self-portrait

420

421 Go out and send a letter

422 Make a list of friends you could write to when you get back

423 Play a tune on a rubber band

424 Type your curriculum vitae

425 Plan your retirement

426 Color in the pattern on the facing page with four colors or tints so no two abutting areas have the same color

42

425

426

430

431

427 Write your name and address in mirror writing

428 Swat a fly

429 Do some exercises

430 Go visit your friends in the company and chat

431 Find a secret space and play cards with your friends

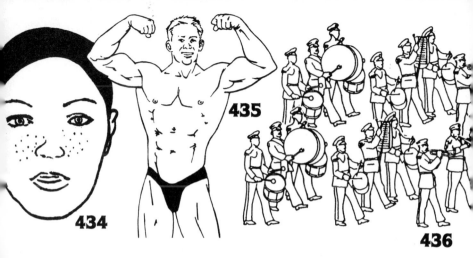

432 Practice the skill of clicking your fingers

433 Toss a coin ten times to see how many times it comes up heads

434 Count the freckles on your face

435 Practice body-building in a mirror

436 Conduct a marching band while humming and chatting

437 Cross and uncross your legs and practice your most impressive sitting position

438 Imagine you are in control of a major operation

439 Each week, look at the backs of your hands for signs of aging

440 Draw circles by tracing around the base of a bottle or cup

441 See how many times you can fold up a piece of paper

442 Make a paper airplane

443 Contact someone on the computer system

444 Roll up bits of paper and throw them at friends

445 Try to remember what is the most you have ever drunk on one occasion

446 Twist around and around on your chair

443

445

In this chapter we cover all weapons that propel a missile and that are fired from the hands or the shoulder without a support. They are personal weapons, wielded by one individual.

We begin with bows and crossbows. In these, although the energy used to throw the missile is still supplied by the firer, it is now stored in the spring of the bow, which was not the case with the simpler sling or spear-thrower.

Then follow the weapons which use gas or air-pressure to propel the missile. This category includes the simple blowpipe and the more complex airgun, although the latter is rarely seen in an effectively lethal form.

453

Next comes the most important category of hand-held missile-throwers: small arms. These are firearms, using explosive force to propel the missile. We have subdivided them according to the simplest functional distinctions, in a way that generally coincides with the historical development of firearms. The chapter ends with some hand-held missile-throwers technically outside the category of small arms. These are mainly large-caliber weapons, now often used to destroy tanks. They are in a sense miniature artillery, and thus anticipate the mounted missile-throwers of Chapter 4.

44

447 Balance on one leg of your chair

448 Write a letter to a famous person who is dead

449 Untangle the telephone cord

450 Calculate how many seconds there are in one year

451 Teach yourself to play the spoons

452 Try to remember what you did this time last year

453 Fill in every letter p on the facing page and avoid reading the text

60 seconds = 1 minute
60 minutes = 1 hour
24 hours = 1 day
365 days = 1 year
450

451

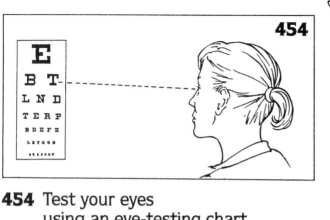

454 Test your eyes
using an eye-testing chart

455 Draw daisies in the margins
of paper or a book

456 Draw boxes and triangles in
the margins of books

457 Polish and shine an old coin

458 Toss a coin in the air as high as you
can without hitting
the ceiling

459 Hammer a nail in the wall to hang your coat on

460 Figure out how to catch the animals that escaped from the zoo

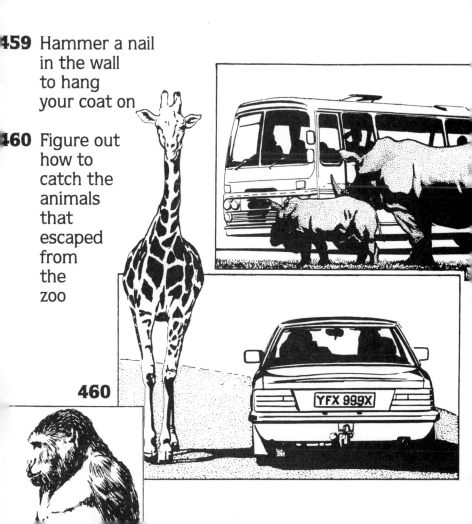

460

461 Clean out your wastepaper basket

462 Think about cleaning your children's bedrooms

463 Photocopy pictures of places you would like to visit from an old history book

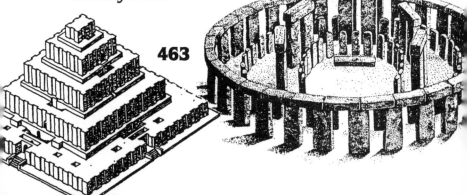

464 Think back to when you last mowed a lawn

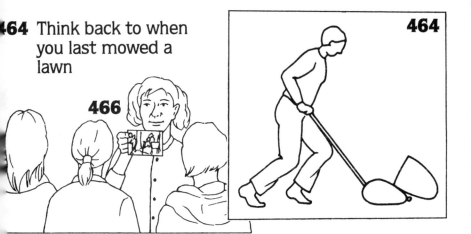

466

465 Try to remember old group photos and the names of everyone in them

466 Ask colleagues to show you photos of their last vacation

467 Make a list of omissions from this list

468 Draw spectacles on photographs in newspapers

469 Figure out what your friends think of you. **470** Figure out what your enemies think of you. **471** Phone a friend and resolve a disagreement. **472** Run naked around the office. **473** Hire a fancy-dress outfit at lunch break and wear it all afternoon. **474** Do skipping with an imaginary rope. **475** Wink at someone across the room. **476** Feed the birds outside the window. **477** Stand on your head and recite your favorite poem. **478** Estimate the cubic capacity of a container. **479** Wear a fancy hat for an hour. **480** Talk to fairies. **481** Greet a new employee. **482** Wake up a friend. **483** Cry to get sympathy from a friend or your boss. **484** Imagine having to migrate to reach a breeding ground.

470

475

472

493

484

485 Dance a jig. **486** Set a clockwork mouse off around the office. **487** Think about looking down from a great height. **488** Show a friend sexy photos. **489** Think about your favorite type of tree. **490** Measure the length of your fingers. **491** Sit on the stairs. **492** Plan a Halloween party. **493** Blow paper at colleagues through a straw. **494** Phone up an airline and find out how much it would cost to travel to London on Concorde. **495** Invent imaginary creatures. **496** Imagine coming to work by elephant. **497** Construct your company's organizational tree. **498** Make a list of the things you would do to your bank manager if you had power over him.

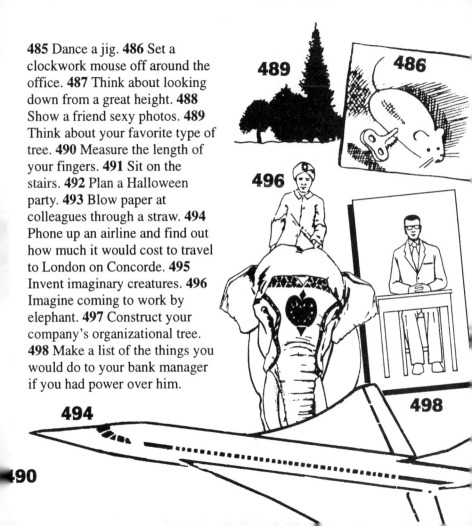

489

486

496

494

498

490

499 Blow your own trumpet

500 Tear an old telephone directory in half

501 Work out number puzzles in your head

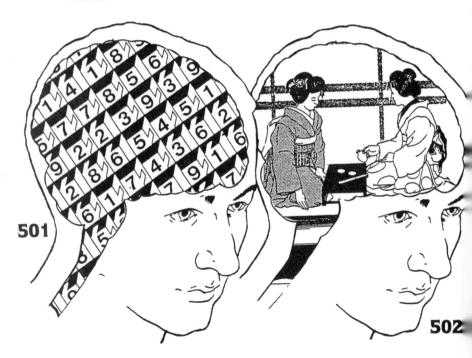

506

505

Once upon a time there was

a . . . . . .

507 Decide what you really want to do with your life

508 Work out the real meaning of life

509 Remember your childhood

510 Learn to calculate

511 Make a list of extinct or endangered species

512 Make a list of everything you ate yesterday

513 Practice juggling

509

511

513

514 Suck peanuts

515 Test your memory by writing down what you did yesterday

516 Write the year in Roman numerals

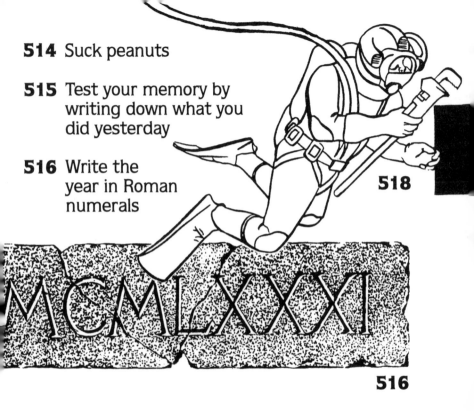

518

516

517 Write your date of birth in Roman numerals

518 Imagine doing a different job

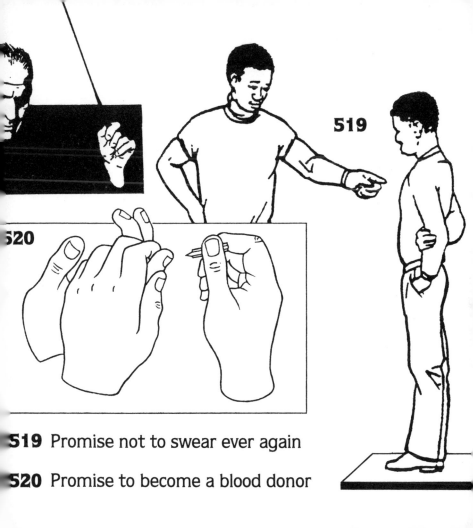

519 Promise not to swear ever again

520 Promise to become a blood donor

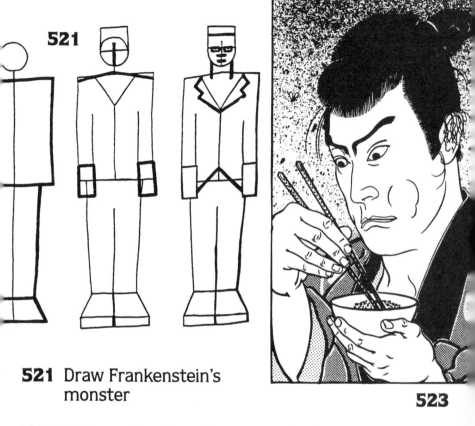

521 Draw Frankenstein's
monster

522 List your ten favorite names for boys

523 Eat your lunch with chopsticks

524 Try to guess the color of objects while blindfolded

525 Imagine ten things you might buy on vacation

526 Practice bandaging your finger

527 Think what you will bring back as presents for friends and relatives from your next vacation

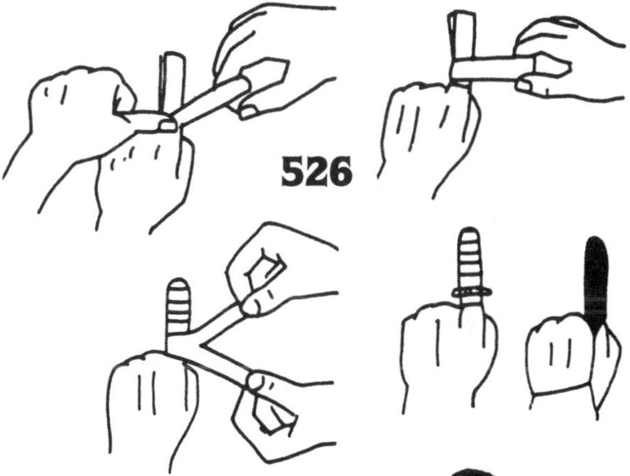

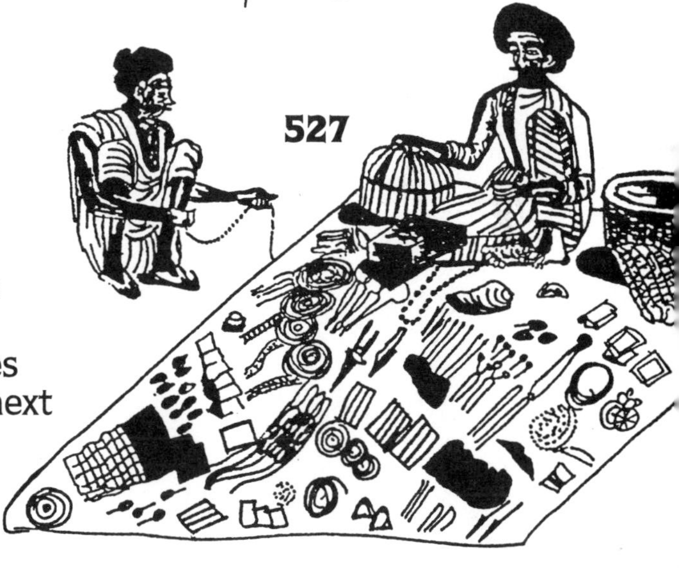

528 Construct a fictitious resumé for yourself

529 Stick *ex libris* plates on your books

530 Imagine wild sexual positions

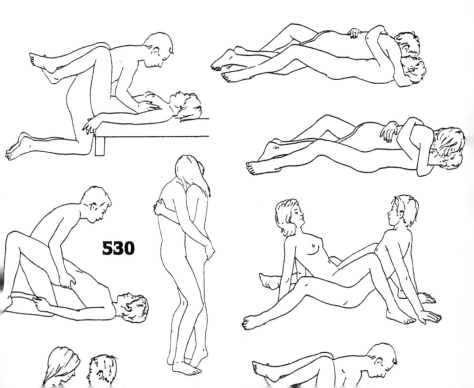

531 List your ten favorite names for girls

532 Polish a peach

533 Practice touching your nose with your tongue

534 Practice touching your chin with your tongue

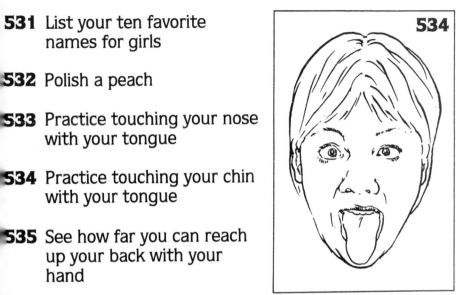

534

535 See how far you can reach up your back with your hand

536 Remember all your old addresses

537 Find out the birthdays of all your colleagues

537

Kyri - July 21st   Bria

Richard - April 9th   Mar

~~~~ June 6th   Bru

538

540

538 Argue with a colleague about who is the best football quarterback ever

539 Remove the dead flies from the lampshade

540 Pick the worst team you can think of in your favorite sport

541 Remove the chewing gum from underneath chairs and tables

542 Write your epitaph

543 Write your obituary

544 Practice telepathy with your workmates

545 Read *Genesis* and give an estimate for the cost of creation

545

BIBLE

546 Imagine how long it would take to write your own biography

547 Look up the value of your old LPs in a catalog

548

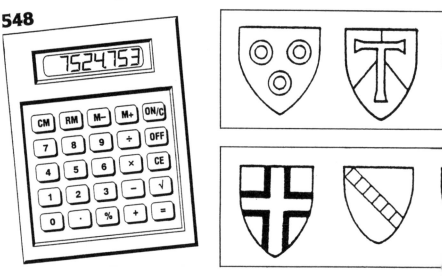

548 Calculate your age in days

549 Name the 101 Dalmations

550 Think of ten reasons why you should get married

551 Devise your own coat of arms

551

552 List your ten favorite actors or actresses

553 Imagine what it would be like inside an iron maiden

554 Conjugate ten verbs

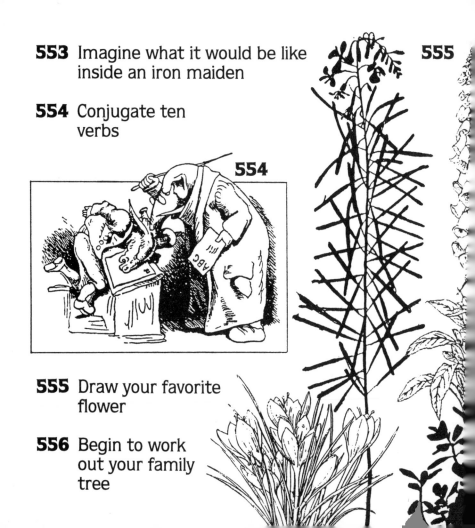

555 Draw your favorite flower

556 Begin to work out your family tree

557 Imagine what you would do if you got your toe stuck in the bathtub faucet

558 Invent a motto

559 Make facial expressions in a mirror

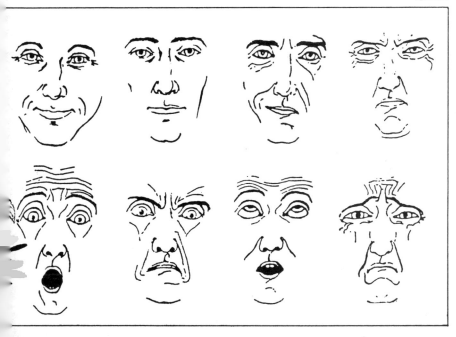

560 Imagine having a life as short as that of a butterfly

561 Figure out what you would do locked in the bathroom without toilet paper

562 Think of a famous person you would like to draw or interview

563 Guzzle a pint of beer

562

560

56

564 Guess who will be the next U.S. President

565 Figure out how you would teach a bear to dance

566 Imagine yourself in women's clothing (if you are a man)

565

566

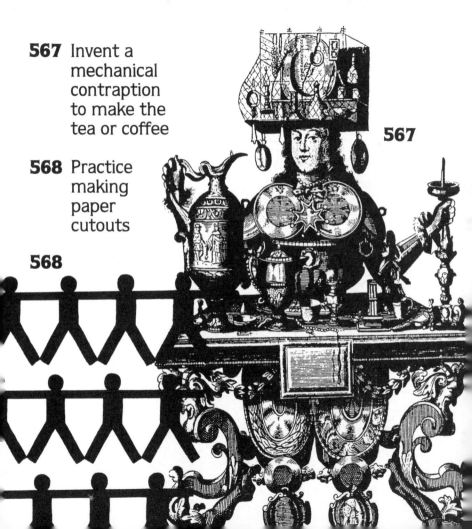

567 Invent a mechanical contraption to make the tea or coffee

567

568 Practice making paper cutouts

568

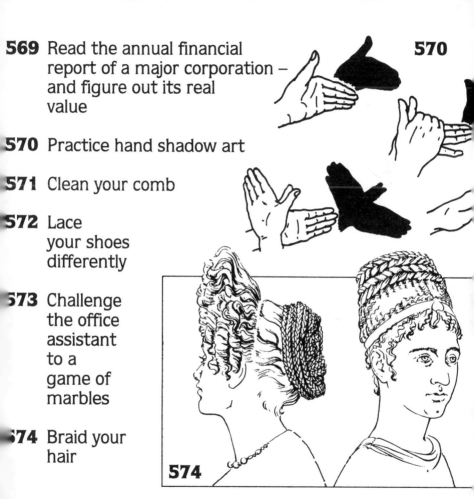

570

574

575

576

575 Imagine how long it
would take to get
to work on a horse

576 If you could return to earth as a
celebrity, who would you be?

579

577

577 Think up the most unlikely business trip

578 Create a new cocktail for the office Christmas party

579 Try to remember what you are supposed to be doing

578

580 Cut yourself some shoe liners from old cardboard

581 Throw things at people from your office window (then hide)

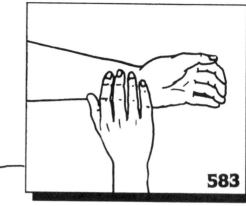
583

582 Measure your height

583 Take your pulse

584 Blow up a paper bag and burst it behind a friend

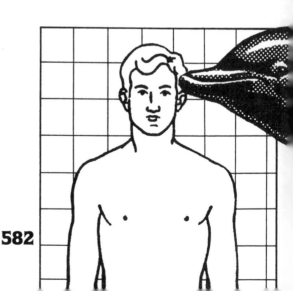
582

585 Surprise someone at work you don't know by taking them a cup of coffee or tea

586 Dream of taking a ride on a dolphin

586

587 Practice blinking with one eye and then the other

588 Arrange your next vacation from work

589 Design yourself a new office

590 Think of a news story for an employee newsletter

591 Design a new chair

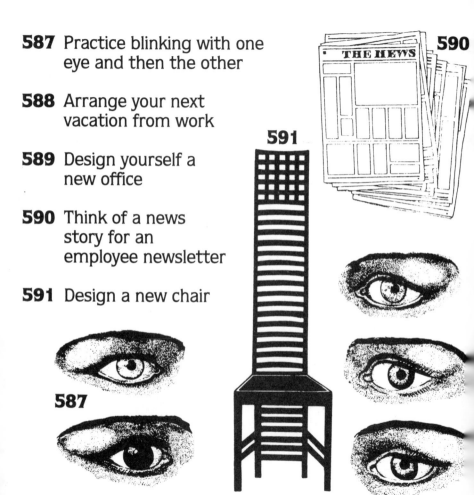

590

THE NEWS

591

587

592 Remember a long-lost relative or friend

593 Wander around the office looking busy

594 Wake up your grandparents with a phone call

593

592

595 Recite the alphabet backward

596 Ask your grandpa what grandma was like when she was young

597 Tie little bits of string into one long piece

598 Plan a trip in a hot-air balloon with your partner

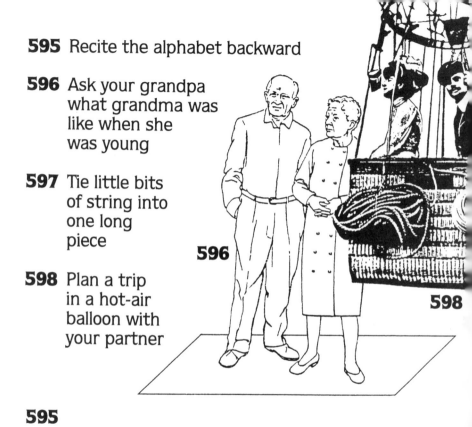

596

598

595

ꓷƎℲGℋℐꓘꓗℒℳ

599 Turn the radio on and find the most boring channel

600 Practice magic card tricks

601 Try to remember old jokes

600

602 Try to remember who told them

603 Write your autobiography in brief

603

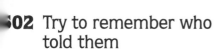

604 Make a machine for blowing smoke rings. **605** Make rude gestures to passersby. **606** Arm wrestle with a colleague. **607** Imagine how to cope with being a werewolf. **608** Make a list of the things you are most afraid of having done. **609** Sit and worry. **610** Sit in as many different positions as you can in the same chair. **611** Panic. **612** Imagine how you would interview your boss for your job. **613** Invent signals that you can send across a field. **614** Talk for hours on the phone. **615** Ask your boss for new office furniture. **616** Make a list of the things you are most proud of having done. **617** Check all the illustration numbers in this book against their captions. **618** Imagine what you would be like as your boss's boss.

605

615

607

613

611

627

ABCDEFGHIJKLMNO

619 Imagine what it is like to have an operation without anesthetic. **620** Practice walking on one leg. **621** Twist the end of an imaginary mustache. **622** Imagine you are floating in space. **623** Write the first paragraph of a comedy or tragedy for the theater. **624** Click your tongue to make a sound like galloping horses. **625** Blubber your lips with your fingers, making bub, bub, bub noises. **626** Try to catch nuts in your mouth by throwing them in the air. **627** Figure out the middle letter of the alphabet. **628** Draw a cyclops step-by-step. **629** Play a tune on your teeth with a pencil or ballpoint pen. **630** Sit and catch people's eyes as they walk by. **631** Invent a secret alphabet and write messages in it. **632** Keep a diary. **633** Rub the rim of a glass until it "sings."

UVWXYZ

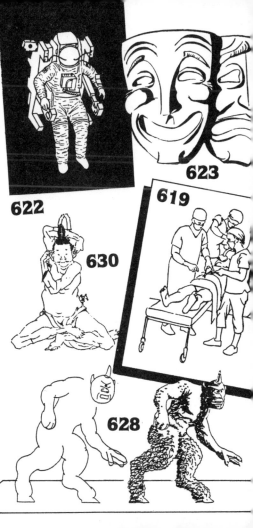

634 Draw a funny picture of your family

635 Watch a sunset

636 Write out your favorite poem as small as you can

637 Think of uses for every room in your own castle

638 Build a house of cards

639 Play solitaire . . . and cheat

640 Spin a coin

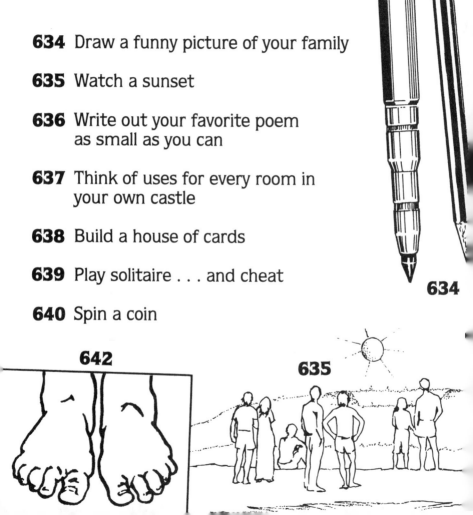

634

642

635

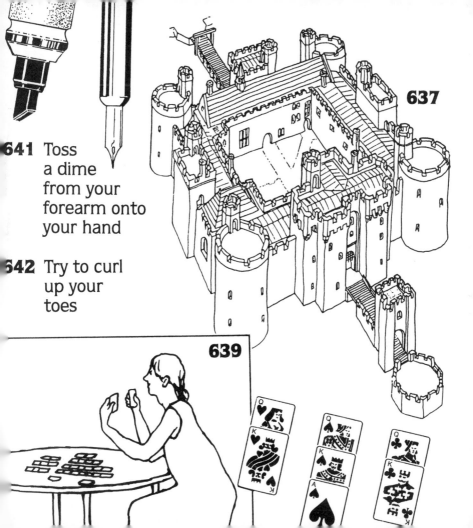

641 Toss a dime from your forearm onto your hand

642 Try to curl up your toes

637

639

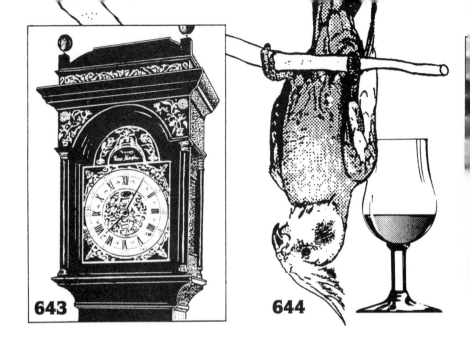

643 Remember where you've seen a large clock (and what time it was)

644 Invent a conversation with a drunk parrot

645 Imagine having to go out and kill your lunch before you can cook and eat it

645

646 Design an old postage stamp

647 Raise your hat to an imaginary passerby

648 Count the typographical errors in a newspaper

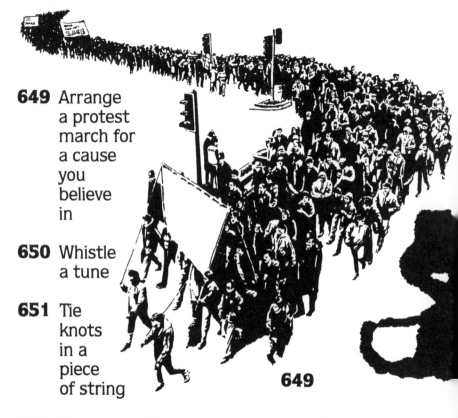

649 Arrange a protest march for a cause you believe in

650 Whistle a tune

651 Tie knots in a piece of string

649

652 Read the obituary column of your local newspaper

653 Scratch your eyebrow with your finger

654 Make ink blots and move them around to form shapes

655 Imagine being a slave asleep on a slave ship

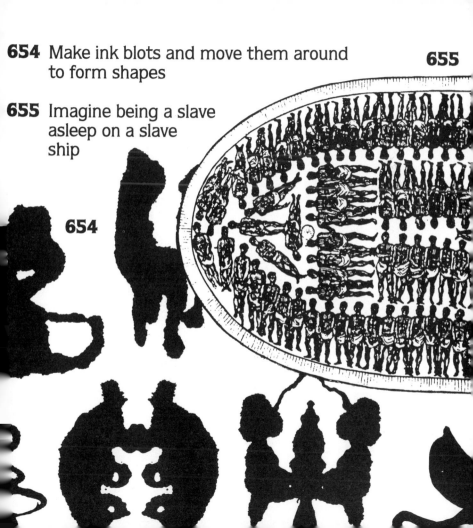

656 Try to add letters to a notice to change its meaning

657 Puff up your cheeks and make squishing sounds with your mouth

657

658 Play with your watch strap

659 Calculate how many minutes you have been alive

660 Imagine what you would do if you had only one day to live

661 Imagine what you would do if you had only one week to live

660

662 Imagine what you would do if you had only one year to live

663 Calculate what you would do if you had a million dollars

664 Check your answers for yesterday's crossword puzzle

665 Draw a map of Europe from memory

666 Invent a wonderful fancy costume

667 Make labels for all the office drawers

668 Call people rude names; then hide

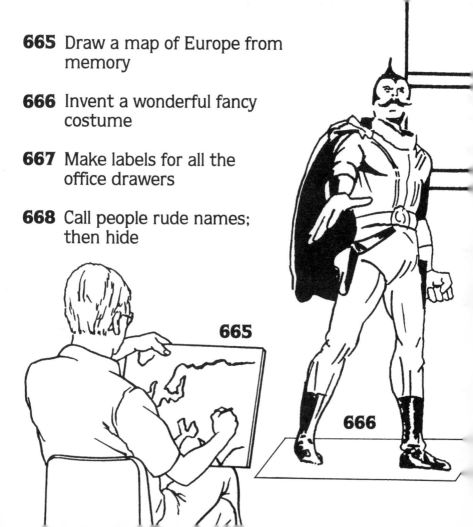

665

666

668

669

669 Make a funny hat

670 Imagine you are making love with Marilyn Monroe (if you are a man)

671 Imagine you are making love with Robert Redford (if you are a woman)

672 Imagine Robert Redford and Marilyn Monroe making love together

673 Sulk

674 Make up anagrams for different countries

675 Calculate how much better off you were last year

676 Draw faces on balloons

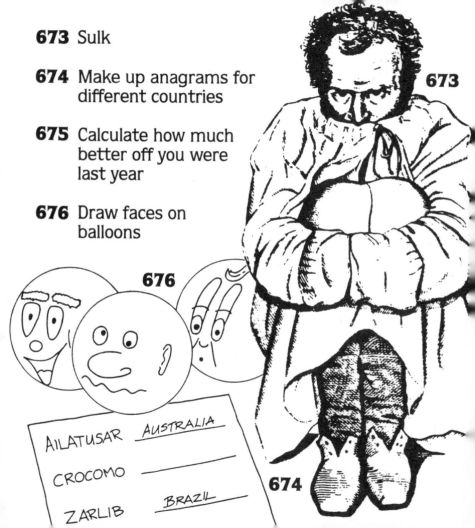

673

676

674

AILATUSAR — AUSTRALIA

CROCOMO — _____

ZARLIB — BRAZIL

677 Think how long it would take you to draw the Bayeux Tapestry

678 Stack up used paper cups and then knock them down

679 Practice belching

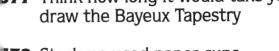

680 Fill in a crossword puzzle without using the clues

681 Imagine a conversation in which your bank manager asks for your help

682 Make a paper chain

683 Look out of the window

684 Annoy a friend

680

681

683

685 Sit facing a blank wall

685

686 Find a new friend

687

687 Remember where everything is in your living room

688 List the faults of your friends

689 Think of a caption for the two pictures below

690 Practice rubbing your tummy and rubbing your head at the same time

689

693

691 Think what you would do if you inherited a mansion

694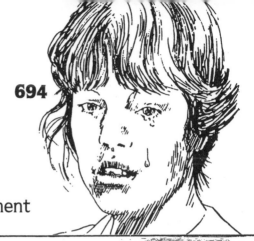

692 Make up a joke

693 Do fifty push-ups

694 Remember a sad moment

691

695 Invent Winston Churchill's next line

696 Go sit on the toilet

697 Design a new office notice board

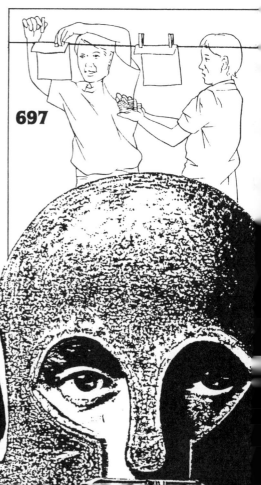

697

695

704

698 Decide which items on your "Things to do" list need doing

699 Make a list in order of priority of the tasks to do

700 Make a list of your debts

701 Decide who you are going to pay this month

702 Stand and sit continually for thirty seconds

703 Imitate other people's way of walking

04 Imagine wearing a fifth-century metal helmet all day

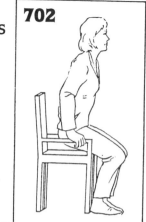

702

703

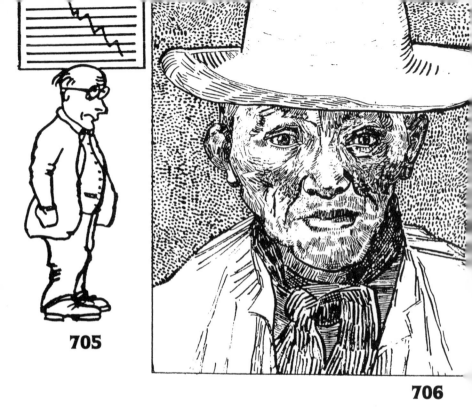

705

706

705 Decide how you are going to pay your debts this month

706 Do a self-portrait using colored pencils

707 Make a musical instrument out of drinking straws

708 Practice signing someone else's signature

709 Write a rude note to your bank

710 Practice writing your name with the hand you don't usually write with

708 *Clan*

711 Invent ten reasons why you would give people medals

712 List a boy's and girl's name for each letter of the alphabet

713 Compare yourself to earlier photographs

714 Make a list of your faults

715 Make a list of your charms

716 Try to move a coin by telepathy

717 Make a list of all the people you owe dinner invitations

718 Tie up your shoelace with only one hand

719 Make silly noises

720 Count how many pages are in this book

721 Imagine the weight of an elephant's suit of armor

722 Pretend you can walk on the ceiling

721

723 Imagine confronting an opponent riding an elephant on the battlefield

723

724

724 Cut out heads from magazines and stick them on other bodies

725 Describe a journey to Britain on an old ship

726 Name Snow White's seven dwarfs

727 Invent a caption for this picture

728 Walk about quickly so you look busy

729 Think what graffiti you would write on the toilet walls

730 Coin a phrase

731 Write a poem

731

732 Stand on one leg for a month

732

733 Eavesdrop

734 Lie very still and pretend to be dead

733

735 Do a jigsaw puzzle upside down

736 Imagine what it is like in Hell

737 Imagine an unlikely place to meet a friend

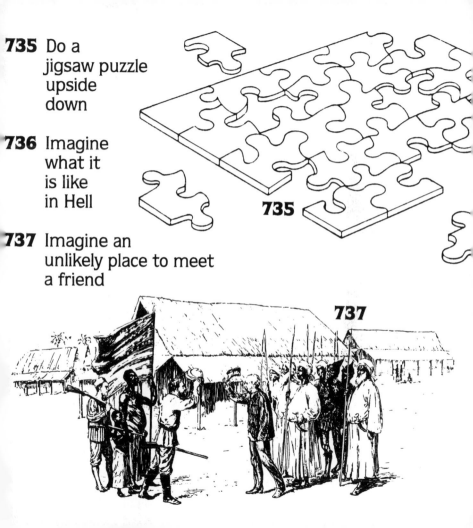

735

737

738

738 Imagine what you would do if you were the richest person in the world

739 Think up an advertisement using a toucan

740 Practice the Mona Lisa smile

741 Imagine a day in the life of a coach horse in nineteenth-century England

742 Imagine what it is like in Heaven

741

743 Massage the bags under your eyes

744 Design a stamp to commemorate your life

747

745 Count television antennas from the window

746 Think of ten easy ways to climb the stairs to work in a suit of armor

748

746

747 Calculate how long it would take you and three friends to build a major road

748 Get drunk

749 Read a book upside-down to see if anyone notices

750 Count the freckles on your forearms

751 Count the roof tiles on the nearest building

752 Imagine what you would do with superhero powers

752

753 Listen to pop music on headphones

754 Chew a match

755 Try to get a dent out of a Ping-Pong ball

756 Imagine whom you would torture if you owned a rack

757 Read every entry in this book, holding it at arm's length

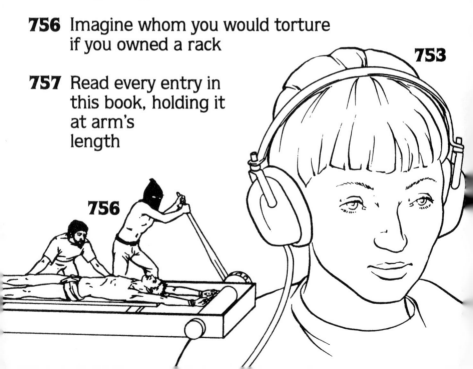

753

756

758 Polish your nails

759 Estimate your total wealth

760 Play a game of gin rummy

760

761 Think of an animal for each letter of the alphabet

761

762 Select a name for your house

763 Imagine being eaten alive

764 Think of five people you would give a medal for bravery

765 Grow a mustache (if you're a man)

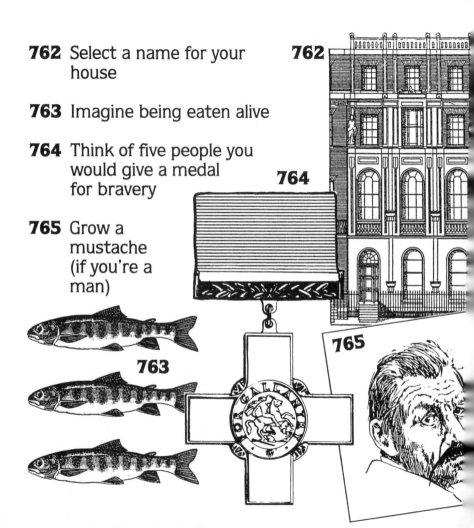

766 Improve your whistling skills

767 Stand on your head

768 Practice drinking from a cup while lying down

769 Cultivate bangs (if you're a woman)

769

767

770 Think of ten ways to cure a hangover. **771** Play cards with a group of workmates. **772** Fill in the teeth on the photographs of people in magazines. **773** Add up a series of numbers . . . your social security number, your date of birth, your telephone number, to see if the total is divisible by seven. **774** Do the same thing and see if it is divisible by three. **775** Learn how to carry out resuscitation. **776** See how many ways you can write the name of the town you live in. **777** Pray for an easier life. **778** Read this book with one eye shut. **779** Watch water run down a window pane. **780** Ask a friend to help you make your own list of wasteful tasks. **781** Try to remember the color of your friends' eyes. **782** Tell someone you just really don't care! **783** Write graffiti on toilet walls. **784** Stomp on plastic cups.

785 Pop air out of the pockets in plastic sheet materials. **786** Run around the office as though someone were chasing you. **787** Build a model of the White House from old cigarette packs. **788** Imagine having to fight for your country hundreds of years ago. **789** Try on hats from the hat stand. **790** Balance a pen, pencil, knife, and fork across your index finger. **791** Find fault with everyone. **792** Demonstrate a karate throw to a colleague. **793** Imagine what you would do if locked in a dungeon for twenty years. **794** Imagine what you would do upon discovering someone you love has died. **795** Imagine for what reason you would want to blow up the government offices. **796** Grow your hair into a new style. **797** Fall into a rage. **798** Master the art of playing musical spoons. **799** Go forth and preach.

786

793

792

776

798

800 Hold your right ear with your left hand and your nose with your right hand, then hold your left ear with your right hand and your nose with your left hand, and repeat and repeat

800

801 Plan what to do with the money when you win the state lottery

802 Think of a job you would not like to do

802

803 Make up a nonsense conversation to have with a friend

804 Make a Christmas card list of friends

805 Clean your hairbrush

806 Imagine having a conversation with Jesus

807 Evaluate how much spare time you have each week to do nothing

808 Learn to draw an equilateral triangle

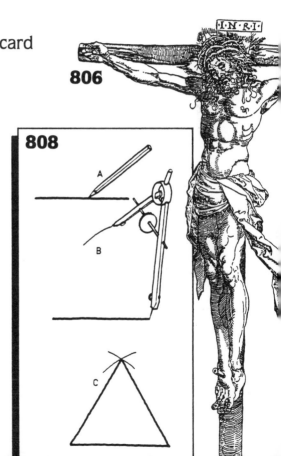

809 Pull off the petals of a flower reciting "she loves me – she loves me not"

810 Learn to identify pasta types

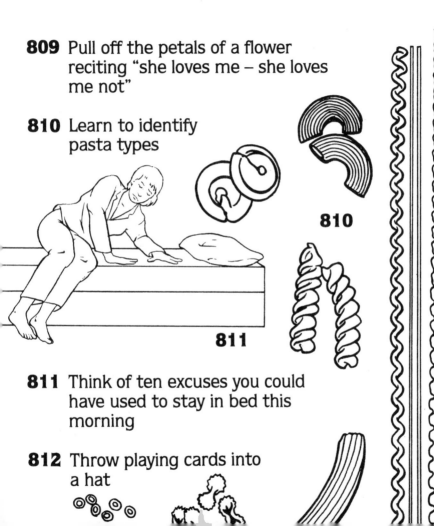

810

811

811 Think of ten excuses you could have used to stay in bed this morning

812 Throw playing cards into a hat

813 Tidy your work area

814 Write down ten reasons why you belong to your religion (if you are religious)

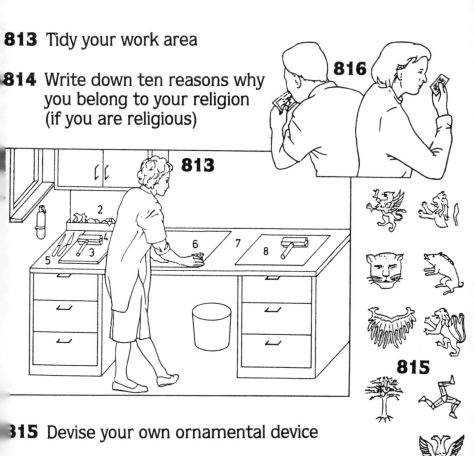

815 Devise your own ornamental device

816 Check to be sure your money is not counterfeit

817 Think of a different thing you could do during your lunch break for the next two weeks

818 Practice making strange faces in the mirror

819 Play yourself at chess – and cheat

820 Place a collection of new magazines in the bathroom for guests to read

821 Think of ten ways to get away with murder

822 March around the office like a Roman soldier

823

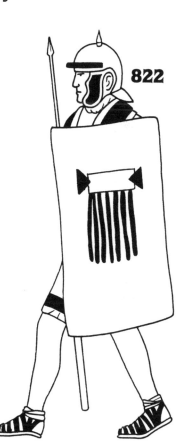

822

823 Write a letter to Santa Claus

824 Exercise your tongue by trying to make it reach the tip of your nose

825 Think where you would like to be buried when you die

826 Learn to read your fortune in the lines on the palms of your hands

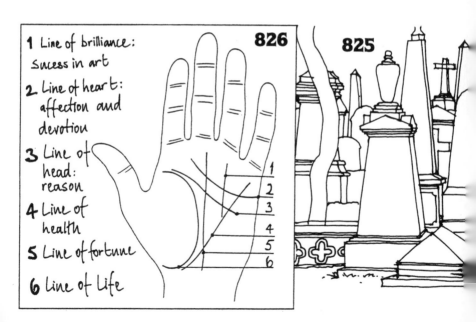

826

825

1 Line of brilliance: success in art

2 Line of heart: affection and devotion

3 Line of head: reason

4 Line of health

5 Line of fortune

6 Line of life

827 Remember your first girlfriend or boyfriend

828 Read all of today's mail again

829 Write a letter to the
Prime Minister of
Britain

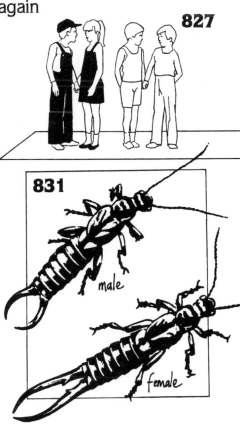

827

829

10 DOWNING STREET

830 Read this book
right through again

831 Learn to identify the
sex of earwigs

831

male

female

832 Memorize the formula for calculating the velocity of water passing through a tube giving the interior distance and the speed

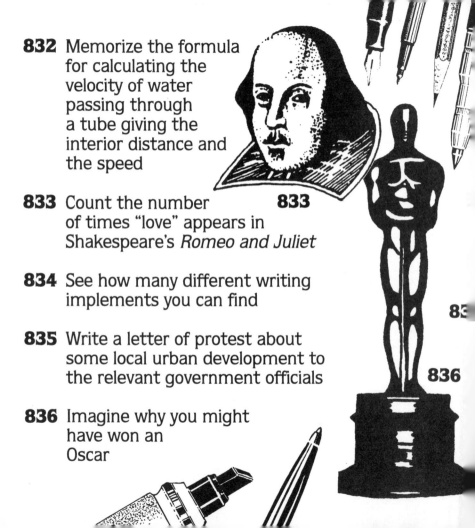

833

833 Count the number of times "love" appears in Shakespeare's *Romeo and Juliet*

834 See how many different writing implements you can find

835 Write a letter of protest about some local urban development to the relevant government officials

8⊐

836

836 Imagine why you might have won an Oscar

837 Search the local telephone directory and call people with the same name as yourself and ask whether they are relatives

838 Imagine playing solitaire in a prison for thirteen years

839 Remove the peel from an apple in one continuous piece

838

840 Build a model Eiffel Tower using toothpicks

841 Learn to identify the names for parts of a sword

842 Count the windows in the biggest building you can see from your window

842

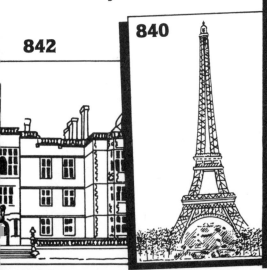

840

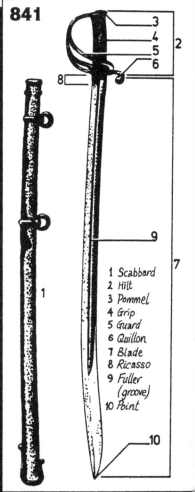

841

1 Scabbard
2 Hilt
3 Pommel
4 Grip
5 Guard
6 Quillon
7 Blade
8 Ricasso
9 Fuller (groove)
10 Point

843 List as many creepy-crawly insects as you can

844 Make shadow images with your hands

845 Jump on your chair and shout "cockroach!" to frighten your colleagues

846 Invent ten new "Old Testament" commandments

847 Figure out how to make a 3-D icosahedron from paper

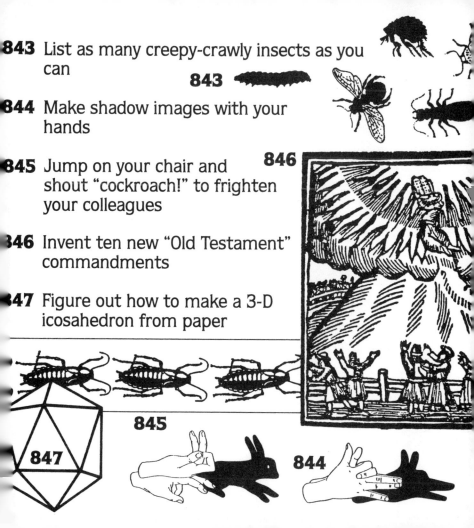

848 Sneak up behind a colleague and try to tie their shoelaces together

849 List all the hotels you have stayed in

850 Avoid stepping on the gaps between sidewalk paving stones during your lunch break

851 Memorize the order of the books in the "Old Testament"

852 Slurp your coffee to distract everyone

853 Count the words on this page

851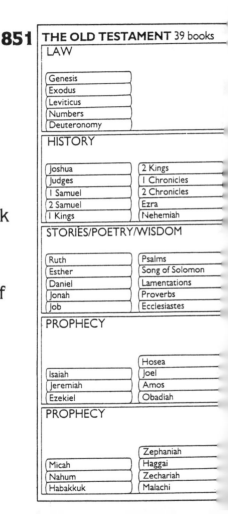

THE OLD TESTAMENT 39 books

LAW

Genesis
Exodus
Leviticus
Numbers
Deuteronomy

HISTORY

Joshua	2 Kings
Judges	1 Chronicles
1 Samuel	2 Chronicles
2 Samuel	Ezra
1 Kings	Nehemiah

STORIES/POETRY/WISDOM

Ruth	Psalms
Esther	Song of Solomon
Daniel	Lamentations
Jonah	Proverbs
Job	Ecclesiastes

PROPHECY

	Hosea
Isaiah	Joel
Jeremiah	Amos
Ezekiel	Obadiah

PROPHECY

	Zephaniah
Micah	Haggai
Nahum	Zechariah
Habakkuk	Malachi

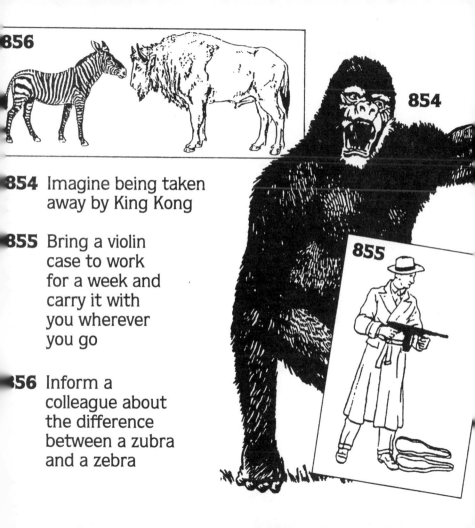

856

854 Imagine being taken away by King Kong

855 Bring a violin case to work for a week and carry it with you wherever you go

856 Inform a colleague about the difference between a zubra and a zebra

857 Improve your ambidextrous skills

858 Imagine being bandaged alive and put in a mummy's coffin

859 Draw twenty circles on a sheet of paper and draw a different face in each one

859

858

860 Get drunk

861 Carve miniature boomerangs from paperboard and flick them at friends

862 Get very drunk

863 Practice drawing perfect circles without a compass

864 Dance around the office with a colleague

865 Imagine having a howler monkey for a pet

866 Sit and stare out of the window

867 Design a new mode of transportation

868 Check share values in an old newspaper (maybe one ten years old) to see what changes have occurred

869 Give up one of your favorite activities for a month so that you feel virtuous

870 Imagine what you would be worth if you had owned some successful shares for ten years

870

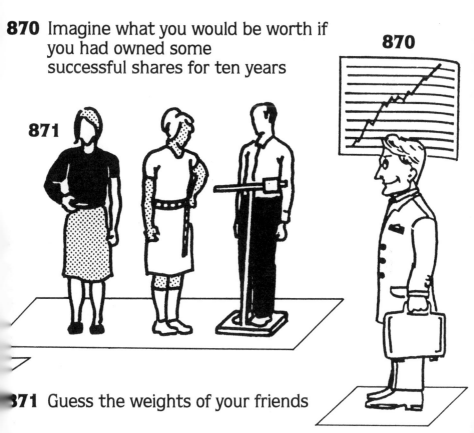

871 Guess the weights of your friends

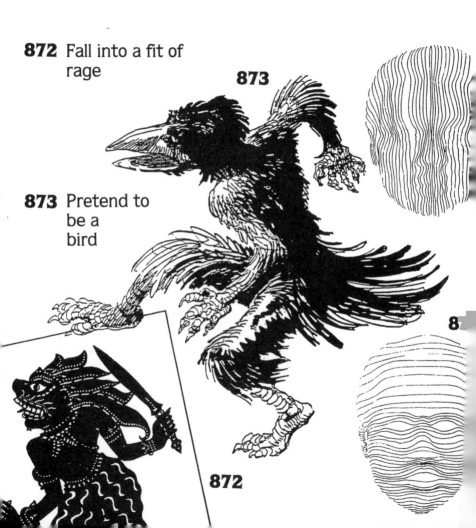

872 Fall into a fit of rage

873 Pretend to be a bird

873

872

874 Imagine what excuses you would make if caught in an embarrassing position

875 Write to the author of this book

876 Draw lines across the contours of faces in magazines

877 Challenge a colleague to a plant-growing race – see who can grow the tallest plant in three months

878 Cover a sheet of paper with doodles

879 Fax a list of jokes to a friend

875

Dear

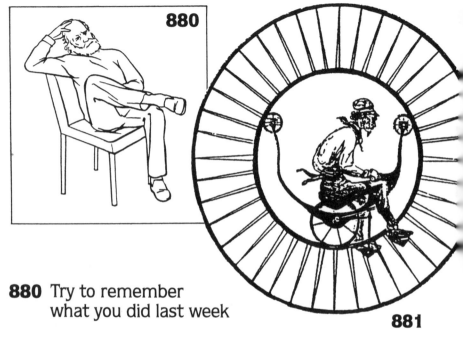

880 Try to remember
what you did last week

881 Imagine coming to work on your
own one-wheeled invention

882 Feel very angry about some
trivial problem and talk about
it endlessly to friends

883 During a phone conversation tell your loved one how devoted you are

884 Imagine coming to work in a tank

885 Measure the height of the plant by your desk

886 Read Ludwig Wittgenstein's *Tractatus Logico-Philosophicus*

887 Discuss Ludwig Wittgenstein's *Tractatus Logico-Philosophicus* with a workmate

882

885

884

888 Imagine what you would say in a message to space, trying to contact alien species

889 Think what you would do if you lost your job

890 Bore your friends by explaining how to draw an equilateral triangle that contains three right angles

891 Imagine Ginger Rogers inviting you to dance and waltz around the room

892 Imagine what you would do if you were very, very ugly

893 Count your blessings

894 Make a list of time-wasting activities

888

is there anybody out there
is there anybody out
is there an

889

895 Talk to angels. **896** Imagine arriving for work in the U.S. President's car. **897** Try to remember who won old national sports events. **898** Check your waist measurement. **899** Laugh at old photographs of yourself and colleagues. **900** Play yourself at tick-tack-toe. **901** Count the number of matches in a box. **902** Think of the ten most beautiful women in the world. **903** Pull up your socks. **904** Work out what percentage of your salary you spend on going to work. **905** Think of the ten most handsome men in the world. **906** Draw cartoons. **907** Doodle. **908** Imagine how cold it must be to wear a kilt in winter.

896

904

908

907

909

89

JENN

DEBB

909 Learn the symbols for the signs of the zodiac. **910** Catch a cigarette in your mouth. **911** Chew a toffee. **912** Guess the value of a dollar in a year's time. **913** Smoke a cigar. **914** Pray for something good to happen. **915** Write a limerick. **916** Imagine being a character in a novel. **917** Design a new desk. **918** Design new office shelving. **919** Cut out pictures from magazines. **920** Meditate. **921** Design an outfit for an office toga party. **922** Try to remember with how many airlines you have flown. **923** Draw a map of your town. **924** Imagine what you would do with $100,000.

922

915

921

919

920

911

925 Construct a theory for the location of your soul

926 Imagine utter despair

927 List what you would do if you had only ten minutes to live

928 List what you would do if you had only ten days to live

929 Pretend you have lost your memory

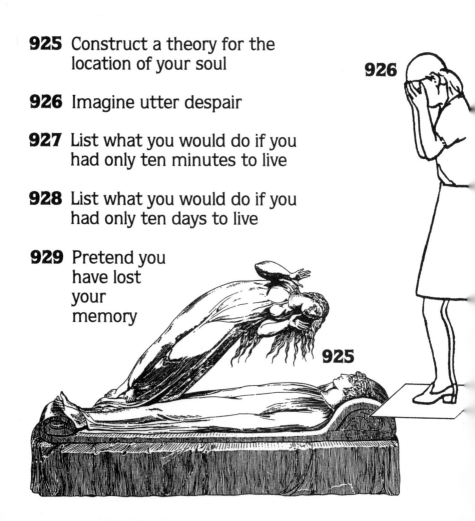

930

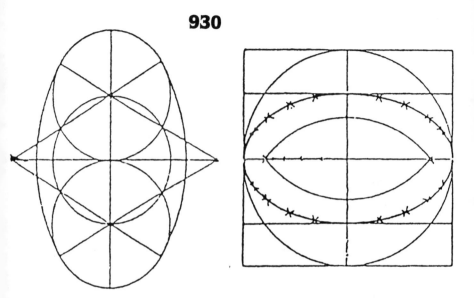

30 Construct elaborate geometric patterns, then color them in with colored pencils

31 Imagine what you would say to the Devil if you went to Hell

32 Imagine being very poor

933 Imagine zero gravity

934 Try to remember who taught you chemistry in college

935 Talk to a colleague about your favorite schoolteachers

936 Make a paper box

933

936

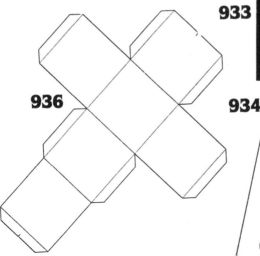

934

(9,1) $CuSO_4 + 2AgNO_3 \rightarrow$
(9,1) $BaCl_2 + 2AgNO_3 \rightarrow$
(10,1) $NH_4Cl + AgNO_3 \rightarrow$
(3,2) $Na_2S + H_2SO_4 \rightarrow H$
$+ 2H_2SO_4 \rightarrow$
(9,2) $BaCl_2 + H_2SO_4 \rightarrow Ba$
(7,3) $2HCl + Na_2S \rightarrow H_2S$
(8,3) $CuSO_4 + Na_2S \rightarrow Cu$
(9,3) $BaCl_2 + Na_2S \rightarrow BaS$
(8,4) $CuSO_4 + 2NaOH$
(9,4) $BaCl$

937 Play with the things on your desk

938 Find a place to lie down in peace

939 Imagine an X-ray of your hand

940 Eat a candy with a noisy wrapper

941 Play with the candy wrapper while
you eat the candy

939

$2Na^+ + 2NO_3^-$
$+ 2NaNO_3 + H_2O$
$a^+ + NO_3^-$
NO_3^-
$+ NO_3^-$
$Cu^{++} + 2NO_3^-$
$^{++} + 2NO_3^-$
$^+ + NO_3^-$
SO_4^-
$H_2O + 2Na^+$
$- 2H^+$
Cl^-
Na^+

938

942 Fall asleep at your desk

943 Figure out who is the tallest in your office

942

943

944 Write your name on your office cup

945 Start an argument with colleagues

946 Scribble on an old fax

947 Stand on your desk and wish everyone a "Good morning!"

948 Figure out who is the shortest person in the office

949 Break your diet

950 Figure out the height of your office building

951 Sit at a colleague's desk while they are not there

952 Sit on the floor

953 Wait until your boss leaves, then blow a raspberry

954 Practice folding your suit jacket for your next business trip

955 Look to see what colleagues are wearing on their feet

956 Find out who borrowed your scissors and get them back

955

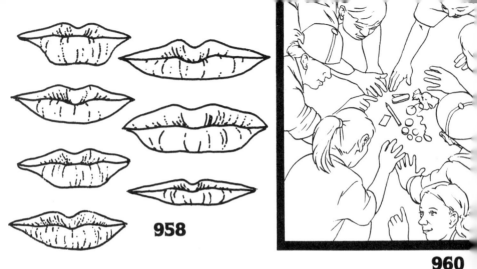

958

960

957 Borrow something from someone and
forget to return it

958 Draw different types of lips and
match them to workmates

959 Get everyone in the office to swap desks
to confuse your boss

960 See who has the most money in their
pockets and make them buy lunch

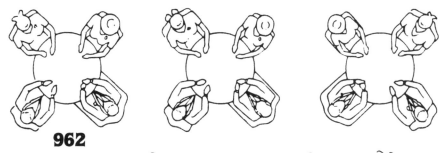

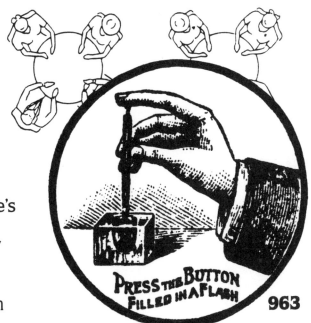

961 Calculate your annual budget

962 Arrange a seating plan for the office's Christmas dinner party

963 Refill your fountain pen

964 Make a mask out of a piece of card or paper

965 Remember the last time you won money at cards

966 Read a newspaper

968

967 Snarl at someone you dislike

968 Imagine how you would look after being told you have got a raise

965

969 Imagine how you would look after being told your raise doubles your salary!

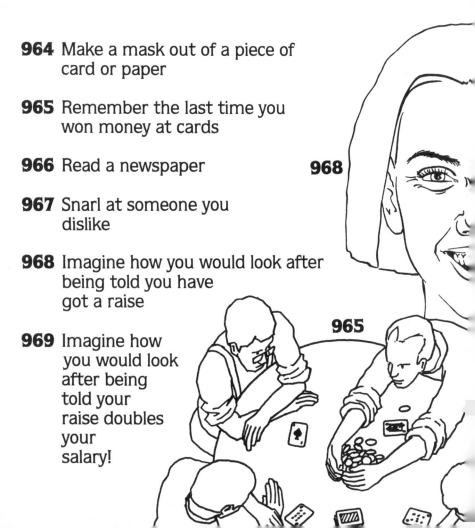

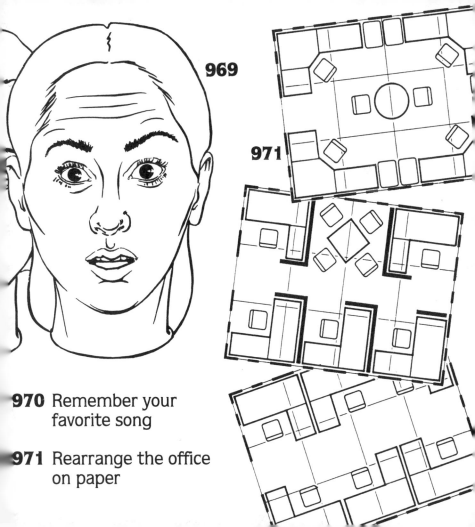

969

971

970 Remember your favorite song

971 Rearrange the office on paper

972 Sing your favorite song

973 Remember last Friday's hangover

974 Calculate which way is north of where you sit

975 Plan a day when you stay at home sick and lie in bed and do nothing

976 Remember your last train journey

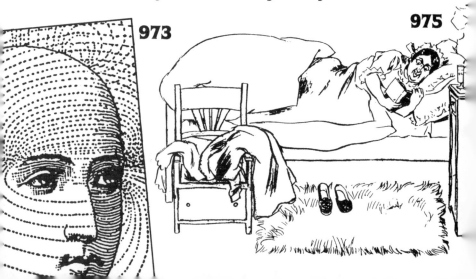

77 Imagine being Adam and what you would have done on meeting Eve

78 Talk to a friend about a problem at home

79 Imagine being Eve and what you would have done on meeting Adam

979

980 Remember an embarrassing moment as a child

981 Remember a special day

982 Remember the age when you first wore a bra

983 Think of ten ways to get into a castle unnoticed

984 Plan to achieve an ambition

985 Tell a friend what happened over breakfast

986 Imagine the worst thing that could happen to you

987 Despair!

988 Do a magic trick in front of your colleagues

989 Throw all your problems at someone else

990 Send messages to colleagues via your computer

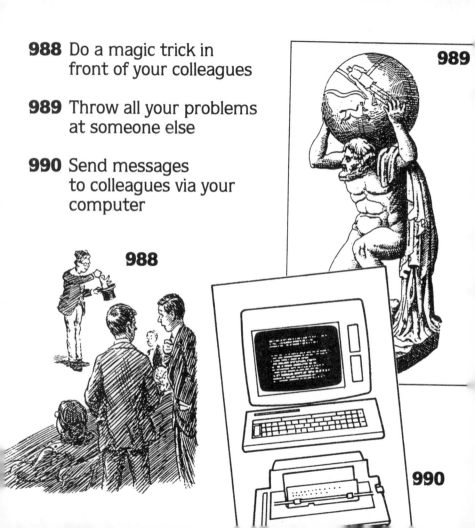

989

988

990

991 Write down all the people that you really care about

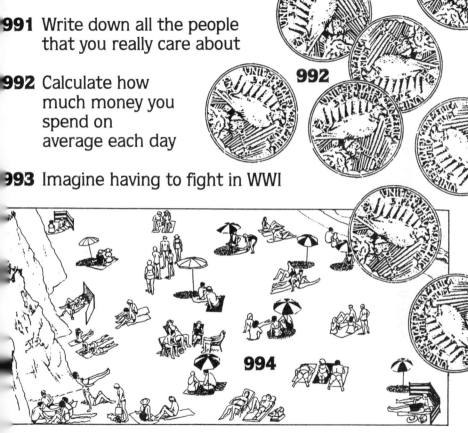

992 Calculate how much money you spend on average each day

993 Imagine having to fight in WWI

994

94 Plan a day at your favorite beach

995 Imagine having to fight in WWIII

996 Imagine having your boss just where you want

997 Make rude hand gestures

998 Remember what you looked like when you were young

999 Write to the author of this book and thank him for wasting your time

000 Laugh at your boss's latest demands

001 Think of the reason why there are 1002 entries in this book

002 Remember items in this book that have been repeated

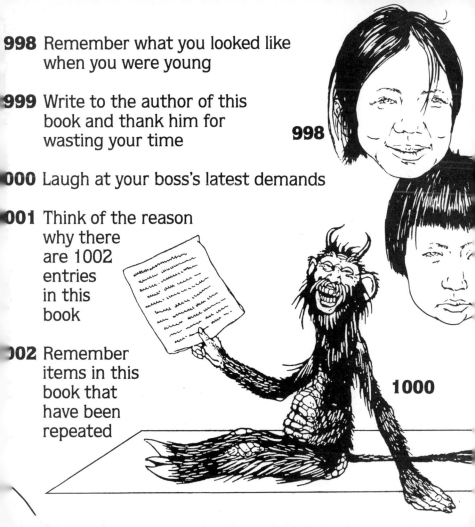